Reality Bites

A NEW WINDMILL COLLECTION
OF NON-FICTION & MEDIA TEXTS

EDITED BY SARAH MATTHEWS

heinemann.co.uk

✓ Free online support
✓ Useful weblinks
✓ 24 hour online ordering

01865 888058

Heinemann Educational Publishers
Halley Court, Jordan Hill, Oxford OX2 8EJ
Part of Harcourt Education

Heinemann is the registered trademark of
Harcourt Education Limited

Selection, introductions and activities © Sarah Matthews, 2003
First published 2003

08 07 06 05 04 03
10 9 8 7 6 5 4 3 2 1

British Library Cataloguing in Publication Data is available
from the British Library on request.

ISBN 0 435 12878 7

Photos: p9 Rex Features/ Charles Sykes; p15 Corbis/Bettman; p32 Mary Evans
Picture Library; p85 RSPCA/Malie Rich-Griff; p88 Popperfoto/Reuters;
p109 Rex Features/SNAP (SYP); p119 Kobal Collection; p150 Panos/Giacomo
Pirozzi; pp167,169, 171 Captive Animals' Protections Society; p172 Crown
Copyright/Graeme Main and Steve Dock; p174 Panos/Jean-Léo Dugast;
p188 Popperfoto/Reuters/Ognen Teofilovski; p197 Microsoft Corporation
from the game 'Amped: Freestyle Snowboarding'.
Cover design by Forepoint
Cover photo: © Getty/Stone
Typeset by Tek-Art

Printed and bound in the United Kingdom by Clays Ltd, St Ives plc

Contents

Introduction for students

Non-fiction and media texts are all around us – on billboards, in magazines, in cinemas, on the Internet – the list could go on and on. But they are not all the same – some are intended simply to give you information, some to persuade you to buy something or to support a cause, some to argue a point of view, some to comment on an event or experience. This book is intended to give you a cross-section of a full range of those texts, from an advertisement for a baby alarm to a screenwriter offering an insight into the choices made when putting together a film.

In order to help you make sense of the variety of writing on offer, and to give you models for your own writing, the texts in this book have been divided into sections depending on the purpose of the writing. When you come across any text, in order to understand it, you need to be aware of three things – why it has been put together, who it has been put together for, and what reaction it is trying to get from the reader or viewer. Those are the questions you need to ask yourself every time you come across a new text: Why? Who for? And what reaction? Every purpose has its own kind of rules for presentation and its own use of language, from the clear, precise language of instructions to the evocative, sometimes flowery language of descriptive writing.

As you study the texts in this book, and carry out the activities associated with them, you will encounter a range of thinking and attitudes, some of which you will find informative, some funny, some thought-provoking – and many, I hope, enjoyable ...

Sarah Matthews

Introduction for teachers

The texts in this book are intended to provide material for both the reading and writing components of the GCSE English examinations, while also providing opportunities for assessed oral work. They have been divided according to the National Curriculum triplets (excluding writing to imagine, explore and entertain, which can be studied more readily in relation to fiction writing), and are also linked thematically to facilitate students' writing about two or more texts.

Each section of the book deals with a different writing purpose, from writing to inform to writing to advise, and each section contains texts which range from the easily accessible to the sophisticated and challenging. The themes, too, provide potential for differentiation, with some, such as childhood and growing up, providing material to which young adults can readily respond, while others, such as war and social issues, deal with topics which some students might find less easily accessible. The range of topics included also provides opportunities for the discussion and increased understanding of moral, ethical, social and cultural issues.

Each genre of writing is accompanied by activities to be carried out before, during and after reading. The preparatory 'before reading' activities are intended to focus students' attention on the demands of the particular genre, either through brief oral discussion, or through a more structured oral task appropriate for assessment. The 'during reading' activities aim to support and direct students' understanding of the texts and of the genre under consideration. The 'after reading' activities are of two kinds. The first set are short, thematically-linked questions which can be used for classwork, homework, or under timed conditions for exam preparation, addressing in particular the requirements of AQA Specification A papers. The second set of 'after reading' activities is intended to provide opportunities for more substantial pieces of extended writing, and target the requirements of AQA Specification A coursework.

The texts are drawn from a wide variety of sources, ranging from textbooks to the Internet, and all the sources are shown on the contents pages at the beginning of the book, each sub-section and in the introductions to the texts themselves. The grid which follows on page ix shows how the texts link together by genre and theme.

Sarah Matthews

What the texts cover and how they fit together

	Childhood	Nature	Travel	Occupations	Science & Technology	Romance	Growing up	War	Choices	Social issues
Inform	'Children in Poverty'	'Look – A Dinosaur!'	'Mongols and Mare's Milk'	'She's Real'	'Patently Good'	'Brand-New Bodies'		Holocaust Resources	'Student Legal Rights'	'School Bullying Policy'
Explain	'Mummy's Having a Baby'						'Growing Up and Your Feelings'		'Making Choices'	'It's Not Always the Greatest'
Describe	'The Matron'	'Far From Shore'	'Jade Eyes'	'The Witch'		'A Chronicle of Love'		'The Girl in the Red Dress'		'Into the Lion's Den'
Analyse	'TV for Toddlers'	'Going with the Floe'			'Et in Arcadia Video'	'Being 100 per cent sure'	'The Challenge to Family Life'	'Making *Welcome to Sarajevo*'		
Review	*Pants*: My New Book'		'New Theroux'	'Inside Advertising'	'Science Books for Children'			'Romancing the Holocaust'		
Comment	'Victoria Climbié'			*The Political Animal*	'Grey Goo'				*Sixth Form Choices*	*Losing It*
Argue	'Mother's Little Helpers'					'In Defence of Romance'	'From Crisis to Coping'	'Oxford for Peace'		'Supermarkets are bad for your health'
Persuade	'Why Cry?'	'Animal Circuses'	'Myanmar Today'			'Loving Yourself'		'Jobs in the Army'		'Work This Out'
Advise		'Beware of the Geese!'	*Mongolia: A Travel Survival Kit*	'Land Your Dream Job'	'Plastic Pollution'	'Give the GIFTS Avoid the Gaffs'				'Are You Being Bullied?'

Section 1

Writing to inform, explain, describe

Although there are similarities between the three different kinds of writing included in this section, and sometimes they can be seen as shading into each other, there are nevertheless important differences between them. This can be seen most usefully as a difference in *purpose*: in writing to inform, a writer's main purpose is to tell you the facts about something; when writing to explain, a writer is trying to tell you about how or why something is as it is, while in writing to describe a writer is trying to help you, the reader, experience something. The definitions below may help you to pinpoint the characteristics of each of these different kinds of writing.

Writing to inform: At first sight, writing to inform is the most straightforward kind of writing that you can encounter – the writer's aim is simply to tell you the facts about a particular topic, while keeping their own attitudes and feelings about the topic very much in the background. Because of this, information writing tends to use fewer describing words, adjectives and adverbs than other kinds of writing, and, where comparisons are made, these are made to help to clarify the reader's understanding rather than to conjure up an atmosphere or trigger a particular response.

Writing to explain: The texts in this section are all concerned with explaining something – an activity, a feeling, an attitude, a way of behaving, etc. This means that to some extent the writers of these texts can all be seen as experts on the topics they are writing about, not only saying *what* something is, but *why*, and, sometimes, what to do about it.

Writing to describe: The writers in this section are all concerned with describing something, with trying to make an experience come alive for their readers, so that they can understand and share what was seen and felt. The whole range of a writer's tools, all the adjectives and adverbs, subordinate clauses and action words, variety in sentence structure and in the length of paragraphs are used to help the reader get a sense of what the writer has experienced.

Writing to inform

Extract 1.1: 'Brand-New Bodies' by Nick Arnold

In this short extract from *The Body Owner's Handbook*, one of the books in the popular *Horrible Science* series, Nick Arnold is concerned with giving the facts about human reproduction in a clear, humorous and easily accessible way.

BRAND-NEW BODIES

Human bodies do more than walk and talk and pee and poo and sleep and dream. They're also designed to produce *more* human bodies. Just think about it! You may own a TV, but I bet it can't turn into *two* TVs! And that automatic bum-scratcher isn't going to make you a new one in a million billion years. But human bodies are actually *designed* to make brand-new human bodies, or babies as they're commonly known! ·

Of course, this is very technical and advanced stuff for body owners, but fortunately we have our experts to guide us. The Baron has just built a baby out of body bits. He's calling her 'Little Monster'. Here she is now with her proud creator ...

LITTLE MONSTER, STOP SUCKING THAT THUMB AND PUT IT BACK IN THE JAR WITH THE OTHER BODY BITS...

Of course, body owners shouldn't try to make babies from body bits – you see the body is programmed and designed to do the job without cutting any bodies up.

HOW THE BODY MAKES A BABY

The first thing that happens is that a human body pairs up with another human body. Two adult human bodies are needed (one male and one female – they're often described as parents). It helps if the bodies in question are:

a alive

b in love with one another.

At this point the body owners ask themselves if they're willing to feed the new body and love it and look after it in the years before the brand-new human body (baby) is able to look after itself.

The two adult bodies are fully equipped to make the baby. The female (known as the mother) produces a tiny DNA-containing micro-production unit – an egg. The egg comes from one of two high-tech assembly and storage units called ovaries. The male (often referred to as the father) makes millions of smaller micro-engineered DNA delivery units known as sperm in his testes. Each sperm is designed to carry a copy of the male's DNA to the egg.

Body owners can let their bodies get down to the mingling of sperm and egg with (hopefully) lots of fun and romance and love sensations running in their sensory equipment. But, since 1978, it's also been possible for scientists to do the necessary mixing in a less romantic test tube.

The incredible egg and sperm race

Body owners are sure to be interested in what happens inside the female's body once the sperm gets there. Basically, the sperm do what they're designed to do: swim to the egg. For the sperm, it's a tough long-distance marathon. It's like a full-sized body swimming 160 km (100 miles) – that's 2,000 lengths of a large swimming pool.

Our sperm beats its little tail and races about 400 million other sperm. It's hard work – it takes 1,000 tail beats to get 1 cm (0.4 inches) and so the race takes about 19 hours.

Extract 1.2: 'Policy Statement Against Bullying'

The text below sets out the school anti-bullying policy for an Oxfordshire comprehensive school. The aim of the statement is to be as clear as possible so that everyone reading the policy – students, teachers, parents – can understand it and can know what to do should they encounter bullying.

POLICY STATEMENT
AGAINST BULLYING

BULLYING INCLUDES:

- name calling
- swearing
- pushing
- teasing
- threatening
- hitting
- kicking
- ignoring
- pinching
- biting
- extortion

No form of bullying is tolerated at this school.

It is everyone's responsibility to prevent it happening.

Bullying is taken seriously and all incidents are recorded and appropriate action is taken.

Support by staff and peers is available for both bullies and victims.

Useful telephone numbers are:
- Childline (0800 626000) – evenings only
- Oxfordshire Parentline (01865 726600) – evenings only

The school aims to raise the self-esteem of all pupils and create an atmosphere of mutual respect.

1 The school's response
- Accurate records are kept of all incidents involving bullying
    - pink slips passed to form tutor who records in student's file
    - three incidents in the log book merits year tutor attention
    - year tutor deals with all serious incidents and records problem and action taken in the central bullying file
    - all bullying records to be held centrally.
- All staff must complete pink slips about all bullying concerns.
- For all serious incidents, statements should be taken from those either involved or witnesses and all details kept in the central file.
- Once facts established, the school can use a range of available sanctions. These sanctions are progressive and are displayed in classrooms.
- The school makes expected standards and appropriate ways of behaving clear to pupils.
- Support will be given to the victims and action taken to change the behaviour of bullies.
- The whole curriculum of the school aims to create an atmosphere of mutual respect and understanding.
- Peer group pressure can be used to discourage bullying.

2 Parents
- Parents are encouraged to work in partnership with the school to achieve better relationships regarding bullying.
- Parents should contact the form tutor if they are concerned about either their child's well-being or suspect they might be involved in bullying.
- For serious cases of bullying, parents will be asked to take part in discussion about what strategies should be used and asked to support the action being taken by the school.

3 Students

Students are encouraged to follow the following guidelines. If you are being bullied the following responses should help:

- Talk to someone you can trust, e.g. best friend, teachers, form tutor.
- Try not to show you are upset.
- Try to ignore the bully.
- Walk quickly and confidently even if you don't feel that way inside.
- Try to be assertive – look and sound confident.
- If you are different in any way be proud of it – it's good to be individual.
- If it is a group picking on you, walk quickly away.
- Avoid being alone in places where bullying takes place.
- If you are in danger get away.

You can help to stop bullying in the following ways:

- Don't stand by and watch – fetch help.
- Show that you and your friends disapprove.
- Give sympathy and support to other pupils who may be bullied. It could be your turn next.
- Be careful about teasing people or making personal remarks. If you think they might not find your comments funny then don't say them.
- If you know of serious bullying tell your form tutor. The victim may be too scared or lonely to tell.

Extract 1.3: 'She's Real' by Sylvia Patterson

This text is taken from an article in *The Face* magazine, a magazine about popular culture for young adults. Sylvia Patterson has two aims here – not just to give the bare facts of Ashanti Douglas' career so far, but also to give her readers an impression of what the young star and her family are like.

She's **REAL**

nly 21, Ashanti has already lent her voice to hits for Ja Rule and Fat Joe. It's rumoured that she supplied vocals for many of J. Lo's biggest tracks. Now she's taking on Mary J and Mariah.

'Hi!' chirps the attractive middle-aged woman in the cosy purple tracksuit, strolling into a London hotel suite, all brisk, toothsome, no-messin'-here professionalism, 'I'm Momager!'

Bidding, perhaps, for entry into the US equivalent of the *Oxford English Dictionary*, Tina Douglas is mom and manager to 21-year-old Ashanti, America's latest, dramatically successful bard-of-R&B. Tina 'discovered' her own daughter aged 12, when she demanded she switch the radio off during housework, to be told by a peeved Ashanti: 'That was me!' (singing Mary J Blige's 'Reminisce'). Nine years later, this April, signed to hardcore hip hop label Murder, Inc. as their lone female R&B architect, Ashanti's debut LP set the US first-week sales record by a solo female artist (504,693 copies sold, more than Lauryn Hill's *Miseducation* ...).

Simultaneously, Ashanti was involved in four US Top Ten singles, writing hooks for and appearing in Ja Rule's 'Always On Time', Fat Joe's 'What's Luv?', Jennifer Lopez's 'Ain't It Funny' and her own debut single 'Foolish', with its tidy lyrical observations: *'My days are cold without you/but I'm hurting while I'm with you'*. A sweet, sensuous, delicate vocalist with a gift for catch-all melodies, clearly there's something of a connection happening. 'This,' says Momager, 'is Ashanti's time.'

Right now, Ashanti is where all the exhausted pop stars wish to be – in bed. 'When "Foolish" came out,' she's saying, her 13-year-old sister sitting next to her, the four corners of this room filled by mum, a Security Giant, her make-up artist and British PR, 'it was all, "God, I feel like you're writing my life story, that's my anthem, I've been going through that for two years." What I do is universal.'

Genial, confident and direct, she's also bullet-proof invincible, a 21-year-old who may well embody the truth behind the success-forging process of the modern musical game.

Extract 1.4: 'Patently Good' by Ali MacArthur

In this article from popular science magazine *Focus*, Ali MacArthur has selected a range of the inventions which have been registered over the past 150 years. The interest for the readers lies in the material itself – the writer has not tried to do anything more than present the bare facts.

Before most people had heard of the telephone, microchips and aspirin, their inventors recorded their ideas in patent applications. Ali MacArthur rifles through 150 years of the Patent Office's greatest hits.

One of the problems faced by inventors is being able to prevent a brilliant, and often lucrative, idea from being 'ripped off' or copied. The inventors' protector comes in the form of the Patent Office, an organisation (found just off Chancery Lane, London) which, since 1852, has been providing a formal system of invention registration. Its records are a catalogue of ideas that have changed our lives, gadgets that are now indispensable, and some items that are just plain odd.

The idea that inventors should benefit from their creativity emerged first in fifteenth-century Italy, before spreading to the rest of Europe. The earliest known English patent was granted in 1449 by Henry VI for a method of making stained glass. The patent formed a pact between the creator and state to protect the idea.

Inventing something is far from clear cut, however. Many inventions have a Darwinian-like evolution, with rival inventors vying to come up with new improvements on the previous design. In some cases it is hard to attribute the invention of a product, as we know it today, to any one person. The beauty of a patent is that it captures a moment in time when a technology was spelled out in words and technical diagrams.

What is a patent?

Patents are an agreement whereby the state grants the individual the right to prevent anyone from copying their invention for up to 20 years. In return, it makes public the details of the patent application 18 months after it is filed.

1867 Dynamite
Alfred Nobel, Paris, France
Filed 7 May 1867, GB and US

Swedish chemist Alfred Nobel wanted to mass-produce explosives for use in mining and set out to explore the commercial potential of nitroglycerine. By mixing nitroglycerine with kieselguhr, an absorbent sand, he found that it could be handled safely. He named the resulting dough-like material 'dynamite' and amassed a fortune, which, as his will requested, funds the annual Nobel prizes.

1880 Electric light
Joseph Wilson Swan, Newcastle-upon-Tyne, Northumberland, England
Filed 27 November 1880, GB

English chemist, Joseph Swan, and American inventor, Thomas Edison, disputed who was first with this invention. Swan may have come up with the idea, but Edison drove the technology forward. Both improved the filaments used in the bulbs. When Edison applied for a British patent, a legal battle ensued. It was settled out of court and the two were forced to merge as the Edison and Swan United Electric Light Company.

1901 Vacuum cleaner
Hubert Cecil Booth, London, England
Filed 30 August 1901, GB

Booth introduced the world to an electric-powered machine with a hose fitted with a filter for cleaning carpets. It was not the true ancestor of the conventional vacuum cleaner, complete with a bag, however. But it did cover much of the groundwork, and he was prepared to personally demonstrate his point by putting a handkerchief over his mouth and sucking up dust.

1902 Tarmac road surfacing
Edgar Purnell Hooley, Nottingham, England
Filed 3 April 1902, GB and US

Hooley, the county surveyor of Nottinghamshire, noticed the improved quality of a stretch of road where a barrel of tar had accidentally fallen from a cart. Slag from a nearby blast furnace had been used to cover the sticky tar. Hooley realised that he could put this by-product of an industrial process to good use and sold the patent to another company which continues to thrive today. Tarmac roads are now so ubiquitous that the trademark is erroneously used in Britain to indicate any road surface.

1914 The zip fastener
Gideon Sundback, Meadville, Pennsylvania, USA
Filed 27 August 1914, GB and US

Unless all your clothing is twenty-first-century Japanese couture you will have at least a dozen items that use a zip. After an earlier version of the 'clasp locker' system failed to take off, Swedish engineer Sundback got the zipper to work by trebling the number of teeth and inventing a machine to stamp them out and fix them on a flexible material – thus creating one of the most ingenious and versatile of clothing products.

1923 Television
John Logie Baird, Dunbartonshire, Scotland
Filed 26 July 1923, GB

Unveiled with much fanfare in London in early 1926, Baird's first working television was mechanical. It was quickly usurped by electronic television but nonetheless, during his long career, Baird created a host of television technologies, including the first transatlantic television transmission. Today, 99 per cent of households in Great Britain have TVs, and the medium provides us with information on almost everything.

1947 The computer
Presper Eckert and John Mauchly, Philadelphia, Pennsylvania, USA
Filed 26 June 1947, GB and US

Naming the inventor of the computer is impossible, but the Electronic Numerical Integrator Analyser and Computer (ENIAC) played a big part in its complex history. Although still just a calculator, it was important in proving that vast arrays of electronics could work reliably at 1,000 times the speed of its predecessors. The device was put together by American engineers Eckert and

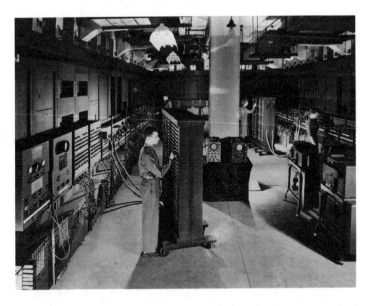

Mauchly and led others to focus on the final step needed to make a real computer: storing instructions in a machine so it could cope with conditional branching.

1958 LEGO
Godtfred Christiansen, Billund, Denmark
Filed 28 January 1958, GB, DK and US

The invention of a Danish toy maker and now a 70-year-old brand, LEGO has been a favourite toy for generations. Over the past 60 years global sales of LEGO bricks have topped £320bn – roughly the equivalent of 52 LEGO bricks for each of the world's six billion inhabitants. It is thought that 80 per cent of European and 70 per cent of American households have some. LEGOLAND theme parks have now been built in Windsor, California, Denmark and Germany.

Extract 1.5: 'Mongols and Mare's Milk' by Tim Severin

The text below is an extract from a book called *In Search of Genghis Khan*, in which travel writer Tim Severin describes his journeys through Mongolia to find the places and peoples from which the legendary king set out on his conquest of much of Asia and Central Europe. In this passage, Severin tells the reader about his visit to a traditional Mongolian *ger*, or tent.

The next day's riding took us through countryside more spectacular than anything we had seen before. The views were positively Alpine, but so unspoiled as to appear as the Swiss or Austrian highlands must have looked 1,000 years ago. Once again the hillsides continued smothered with wild flowers from one slope to the next, so that in the space of a mile we would pass from an area that was purple, to a slope which might be yellow, and then to a third hillside white with so many edelweiss that it appeared from a distance that it had snowed in the afternoon. The flowers came in every shape, from tall spiked columns to tiny blossoms as small as forget-me-nots. For six hours we rode on a flowery tapestry except where our horses had to thread their way around the debris of an ancient lava flow that had oozed down the valley and congealed, leaving a jumbled moonscape of dark brown rocks.

A small lake had ponded up behind the lava flow and here we stopped for our noonday break. A group of four *gers* had been placed close to the water's edge, and the Drunk led us eagerly towards them, knowing the hospitality we could expect. The welcome would be the same at nearly every *ger* throughout our summer ride: we would enter, nibble a little food, and drink vast quantities of mare's milk and alcohol. Gone were the hungry days of boiled mutton and cold thin tea, for now we were in the brief season of high summer when the flocks and herds were giving ample milk, and the Mongol diet was virtually pure milk. To turn away a stranger at such a time of richness was unthinkable. Hospitality was given, and taken, for granted. My own inclination was to hover outside and wait to be invited into a *ger*, but our Mongol companions did not even pause for an instant. They would ride straight to the tether line between its two poles, tie up their horses, stroll over to the largest and most important *ger*, push open the door and walk in as if it were their own home.

The scene inside was always the same. A metal stove, about half the height and the same shape as an oil barrel, stood directly in front of the door with its metal chimney rising up through the smoke hole in the apex of the felt tent. Three or more iron bedsteads were arranged in a semi-circle around the back and sides of the *ger*, and the spaces between them were filled with chests of drawers usually painted orange and decorated with flowery bands. The host's seat was at the furthest point away from the door, and his most senior guest would be placed on his right while the other guests either sat on the beds or made themselves comfortable on the ground within reach of a low table that was set before the host. On the table there was always a dish ready and waiting, piled with sugar lumps, hard biscuits and dried curd. Usually as we arrived the wife would already be stoking the fire to boil up milk and water for salt tea, but *ayrag*, mare's milk, was what our companions wanted, gallons of it. It became clear how the Mongols had earned themselves the nickname 'the drinkers of mare's milk'. The quantities of *ayrag* which our companions consumed were almost beyond belief. It was not unusual to see them drink 17 to 20 pints in a day, and as social etiquette expected every visitor to drink three bowls of milk before leaving the *ger* neither Paul nor I escaped the orgy of milk consumption. The *ayrag* was kept ready, either in a barrel or usually in a leather sack hanging on a frame just inside the door. It was not drunk fresh but half-fermented, so that it had a sour and sometimes slightly fizzy taste. At intervals the woman of the house would take the wooden paddle whose handle stuck out from the milk bag and beat air into the brew with a hollow squelching sound to aid the souring process.

Nothing much had changed since Rubruck's day. Mare's milk, he noted, 'is made in the following way':

'They stretch above the ground a long rope attached to two stakes stuck in the soil, and about the third hour (nine o'clock) tether to the rope the foals of the mares they intend to milk. Then the mares stand beside the foals and let themselves be milked peacefully.

'So having collected a great quantity of milk, which when it is fresh is as sweet as cow's milk, they pour it into a large skin or bag, and set about churning it with a club which is made for this purpose, as thick as the lower end of a man's head and hollowed out. As they stir it rapidly, it begins to bubble like new wine and turn sour or ferment, and they keep churning it until they extract the butter.

'Next they taste it, and when it is moderately pungent they drink it. While one is drinking it, it stings the tongue like wine from unripe grapes, but after one has finished drinking it leaves on the tongue a taste of milk of almonds. It produces a very agreeable sensation inside and even intoxicates those with no strong head; it also markedly brings on urination.'

Extract 1.6: 'UK Tops Europe for Children in Poverty' by Simon Vevers

In this article from the specialist magazine *Nursery World*, aimed at those in the domestic childcare profession, Simon Vevers puts forward the facts about the position of children living in poverty in the UK.

UK Tops Europe for Children in Poverty

The UK still has the highest rate of child poverty in Western Europe, despite overall improvements in children's well-being over the past five years, according to a report commissioned by Save the Children.

The charity's report said that nearly a third of UK children live in relative poverty and the rate has more than trebled in the past twenty years, peaking in the late 1990s. Its publication coincided with Prime Minister Tony Blair's launch last week of the Government's own annual report into child poverty and his pledge to do more to tackle it by 'redistributing wealth and opportunity to the many, not the few'.

Andrew Smith, Work and Pensions Secretary, said 1.4 million fewer children were living on absolute low income than in 1997 and that the Government was committed to cutting the number in low-income households by a quarter by 2004.

The report, *The Well-Being of Children in the UK*, was carried out by researchers at York University, who made a comprehensive study of the physical, cognitive, behavioural and emotional well-being of children by examining issues ranging from poverty, health and education to crime and the environment. It said that while overall child poverty rates remained high, poverty is unevenly distributed. Wales has a higher rate than England and Scotland, but has 'sharp local concentrations', and the ward with the highest proportion of children living in poverty – 96 per cent – is Whitfield South in Dundee, Scotland. Northern Ireland has relatively high rates in all wards.

Calling on the Government to produce its own child well-being report, Save the Children policy and strategy manager for the UK and Europe Madeleine Tearse said, 'It is impossible to imagine how governments can effectively reach the children most in need of their support without detailed UK-wide and country-level monitoring of children's well-being'.

Martin Barnes, director of the Child Poverty Action Group, welcomed the Prime Minister's commitment but said the Government should stop playing 'pick and mix' with poverty statistics by trying to redefine how poverty is measured.

He added that the Government had failed to heed the advice of a Commons committee eighteen months ago that had recommended urgent reform of the Social Fund, and it had failed to introduce a new child-support scheme to help the poorest families.

The Save the Children report also highlighted trends in health. The researchers found that compared with other age groups, the highest rate of increase in the prevalence of chronic ill-health was among children, with obesity, diabetes and asthma all increasing while immunisation rates are down. Children in Scotland have the worst diets but the best educational attainment. Northern Ireland has the highest infant mortality rate, but the lowest teenage pregnancy rate.

Extract 1.7: 'Student Legal Rights'

The article below comes from the website maintained by the *Guardian* newspaper. It reproduces an article published in the *Guardian* at the beginning of the academic year in 2002, telling students how to go about setting themselves up and looking after themselves as they start their new life away from home at college or university.

A ROUGH GUIDE

Student
Legal Rights

Friday 27 September 2002

the Guardian

Arriving at university often means signing your first housing contract, getting a part-time job with dubious rights, and entering a vague contract with a powerful institution – the university. Here is a rough guide to your legal rights, their obligations and how to stay out of trouble.

HOME LIFE

Stories of rogue landlords providing substandard accommodation are rife because they are true. The only way to avoid it is to get your legal head on.

Letting agencies: Agents are not allowed to charge a registration fee for finding accommodation, and can only make a charge when the client accepts it.

- Agencies will often ask for a parent to guarantee a student's rent; it's within their rights, but parents need to seek legal advice before signing, not least to make sure they are only liable for their own child's rent, and not the whole house.

Private accommodation: Landlords demand a deposit – usually one month's rent, but getting that deposit back can be a considerable problem. Landlords legally have to pay you the interest on your deposit when you leave. Basically to get your deposit back, you have to leave the house in the same state as you found it, to make sure of this the landlord should provide an inventory and you should note any damage to the property when you move in. If you think the landlord is unreasonably withholding your deposit, you can take them to the small claims court, a relatively simple process which your student union can help you with. It is free for complaints involving less than £1,000. Increasingly students simply withhold their last month's rent anticipating that they won't get their deposit back. This is illegal.

- Check in your contract what repairs the landlord is responsible for, make sure everything is covered, including the outside drains. It is the landlord's legal responsibility to make sure the gas appliances are safety-checked and that fire alarms are fitted. Try and get an electrical check as well.

- Student occupiers are protected in law from harassment from their landlords. Harassing behaviour includes repeated late night visits, entering the property without permission, changing or adding to the tenancy agreement, ignoring repair work, aggressive attitudes – physical or verbal.

WORKING LIFE

Student finances don't add up. You, along with 96 per cent of your peers, are going to be doing some kind of part-time work during your degree, and it's likely you'll be on temporary contracts, if any, with no holiday pay, no sick pay and no rights against dismissal. Rogue employers know that students are ripe for the picking, so here's what they can't do and what you can expect.

Just because your job may be temporary, part-time, casual or on a seasonal basis, that doesn't mean you don't have any rights. You do.

- You have a right to the minimum wage: £3.50 an hour if you're aged between 18 and 21, and £4.10 once you are 22 and over.
- You have the right to know the terms of your employment, and that your employer adheres to the conditions set out in that. Before two months, this will be verbal and after in the form of a written statement or contract.
- When you apply to a job, and once you're in it, you have the right not to be discriminated against.
- Once in the job you have the right to a written wage slip showing what deductions are being made, working time rights (including holiday pay), and you have the right to equal pay with members of the opposite sex.
- After a month: you can expect one week's notice of dismissal, payment if you are suspended on medical grounds and wages if you are laid off.
- After two months: you are entitled to a written contract.
- After one year: you are entitled to claim for unfair dismissal and can take up to 40 weeks off for maternity leave.
- After two years, you can make claims for redundancy.

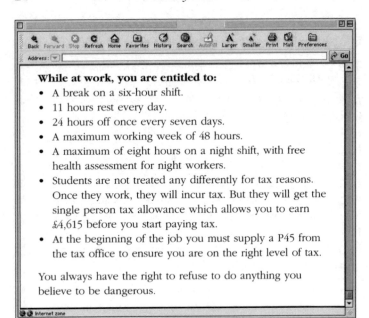

While at work, you are entitled to:

- A break on a six-hour shift.
- 11 hours rest every day.
- 24 hours off once every seven days.
- A maximum working week of 48 hours.
- A maximum of eight hours on a night shift, with free health assessment for night workers.
- Students are not treated any differently for tax reasons. Once they work, they will incur tax. But they will get the single person tax allowance which allows you to earn £4,615 before you start paying tax.
- At the beginning of the job you must supply a P45 from the tax office to ensure you are on the right level of tax.

You always have the right to refuse to do anything you believe to be dangerous.

Extract 1.8: The Holocaust Memorial Resource and Education Centre of Central Florida

The text which follows comes from a website set up by the State administration in Florida in the USA, telling parents, teachers and students about a new piece of legislation requiring students in Florida to study the Holocaust, the massacre of over 6 million Jews by the Nazi regime in Germany during the Second World War. It is interesting to see how some aspects of history or culture are seen to be so important it is thought necessary for students to study them by law. This is what Florida State has done with the Holocaust, and what the National Curriculum in England and Wales did in 1989, making the study of Shakespeare's plays a legal requirement in state schools.

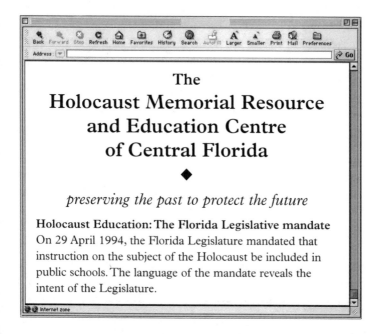

The

Holocaust Memorial Resource and Education Centre of Central Florida

◆

preserving the past to protect the future

Holocaust Education: The Florida Legislative mandate
On 29 April 1994, the Florida Legislature mandated that instruction on the subject of the Holocaust be included in public schools. The language of the mandate reveals the intent of the Legislature.

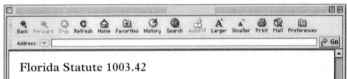

Florida Statute 1003.42

'Members of the instructional staff of public schools, subject to the rules and regulations of the state board and of the school boards, shall teach efficiently and faithfully, using the books and materials required, following the prescribed courses of study, and employing approved methods of instruction the following:

'The history of the Holocaust (1933–1945), the systematic planned annihilation of European Jews and other groups by Nazi Germany, a watershed event in the history of humanity to be taught in a manner that leads to an investigation of human behaviour, an understanding of the ramifications of prejudice, racism and stereotyping, and an examination of what it means to be a responsible and respectful person, for the purposes of encouraging tolerance of diversity in a pluralistic society and for nurturing and protecting democratic values and institutions.'

This mandate does not limit instruction on the Holocaust to any particular grade level or academic subject. Inclusion of Holocaust studies may be spread throughout the curriculum in a variety of appropriate areas. In order to fulfil the terms of the mandate, a comprehensive Holocaust education programme would ideally encompass the following six approaches:

1 A presentation of the history of the Holocaust:

a As a calculated and systematic programme which culminated in mass murder.

b As a turning point in human history.

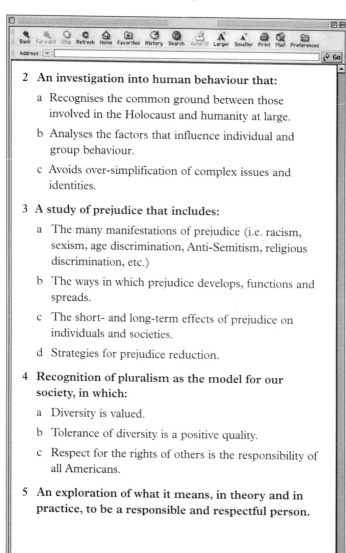

2 **An investigation into human behaviour that:**

    a Recognises the common ground between those involved in the Holocaust and humanity at large.

    b Analyses the factors that influence individual and group behaviour.

    c Avoids over-simplification of complex issues and identities.

3 **A study of prejudice that includes:**

    a The many manifestations of prejudice (i.e. racism, sexism, age discrimination, Anti-Semitism, religious discrimination, etc.)

    b The ways in which prejudice develops, functions and spreads.

    c The short- and long-term effects of prejudice on individuals and societies.

    d Strategies for prejudice reduction.

4 **Recognition of pluralism as the model for our society, in which:**

    a Diversity is valued.

    b Tolerance of diversity is a positive quality.

    c Respect for the rights of others is the responsibility of all Americans.

5 **An exploration of what it means, in theory and in practice, to be a responsible and respectful person.**

6 **An investigation of democratic values and institutions that recognises:**

a The fundamental differences between democratic and non-democratic systems.

b That these values and institutions are sustained only through the continual efforts of concerned citizens.

The Holocaust was an extraordinarily complex period in history. It defies broad generalisations and easy explanations. Some instructional methods that may be well suited for other subjects are inappropriate for the teaching of the Holocaust. Careful thought and planning are needed to ensure historical accuracy and sound methodology. A good Holocaust studies programme will provide students with an understandable and compelling narrative. It should provide a broad view of the subject, while at the same time affording the opportunity to encounter individual lives. It must also place the people and events of the Holocaust in appropriate geographical and historical contexts. Finally, it should offer students plentiful opportunities to reflect on personal and collective applications for the lessons learned.

Obviously, most teachers will not have time to explore all of these issues within the context of a single Holocaust unit. Most will choose to focus on those aspects of the topic most closely related to their course curriculum. Hopefully, students will study about the Holocaust in a variety of classes throughout their years in school and will have many opportunities to learn and apply its vital lessons.

Internet zone

Writing to inform: Activities

Before reading – oral activities

1 Oral activity for access:

    a In pairs or in a small group, brainstorm and note down how many different kinds of information writing you can think of that you come across in the course of a normal week (newspaper or magazine articles, notices in public places, school textbooks, opening times on shop doors, etc.).

    b Discuss what the *purpose* of information writing is, and note down two or three features which you think all these different kinds of writing have in common (for instance, facts).

2 Oral activity for assessment (group interaction – discuss, argue, persuade):

    a In a small group, select a topic on which you all feel fairly expert (a favourite band, a football club, school dinners, etc.). Brainstorm and note down all that you already know about the topic.

    b Imagine that you were going to make a presentation on your topic to the class, informing the whole class about your chosen subject.

    c Discuss and note down what you feel you still need to find out to make your information complete – if you can, think of how you will do this and where you would need to go to find out the additional information (for example, libraries, websites).

    d Talk briefly about how you would make your presentation to get the information across to the class as clearly as possible (charts, graphs, OHPs, etc.).

During reading

1   As you read the extracts in this section, you need to be aware of a number of things:

- the readership the writer is addressing (children, young adults, specialists, general readers, etc.)
- the topic they are writing about
- the facts they are conveying
- the language they use
- their use of layout or graphics.

2   Information writing is, in a way, the most 'invisible' writing of all – it is the topic which is kept centre stage, while the writer fades into the background. But the writer still has choices to make about which facts to concentrate on and how best to present them to the reader.

a   As you read, note down all *facts* that you are given in the extract or extracts you are studying. When you have done that, jot down a few notes on *how* the writer has presented the facts to the reader (for example, using humour, using drawings, making comparisons) and what kind of reader they are addressing.

b   When you have finished making your notes, share them with a partner or in a small group and draw up a final list under four headings:

- the target readership
- the topic
- the facts provided
- the tools the writer has used (you might like to include short quotations or references to the text in this list).

After reading

Select a question from *either* the linked writing *or* the coursework questions at the end of this book and follow the instructions to help you prepare and answer the question.

Writing to explain

Extract 1.9: 'Look – A Dinosaur!'

Taken from the I-Spy book of *Dinosaurs and Prehistoric Animals*, this extract explains two different things – how to use the book, and how the giant dinosaurs lived and what they looked like.

Look – A Dinosaur!

How to use your I-Spy book

You cannot I-Spy a living dinosaur because dinosaurs became extinct 65 million years ago. Many fossils and models of the dinosaurs and prehistoric animals shown in this I-Spy book can, however, be found in museums or theme parks. Over the past ten years, the methods and materials used to construct models have changed a lot, and those driven by motors and covered in a flexible 'skin' are most life-like. Finding skeletons and bones in the field is possible but dinosaur fossils are rare, particularly in the developed countries of Europe. You could probably complete your I-Spy quest with a couple of visits to the Natural History Museum in London. Local museums can be just as rewarding, however, and they may also provide information about areas locally where you might make your own unique discovery.

Giant dinosaurs

The giants of the dinosaur world were the sauropods. These were plant-eating monsters that grew to lengths of as much as 30 metres (100 ft). The heaviest were *Brachiosaurus* and *Supersaurus* weighing in at over 80 tonnes. *Supersaurus* was probably at least 15 metres (almost 50 ft) tall, too!

The sauropods can be divided into two groups, the brachiosaurs and the apatosaurs. Brachiosaurs have long front legs and are tall at the shoulder whereas apatosaurs have long back legs and tend to lean forward.

The Jurassic (208–144 million years ago) landscape was forested with firs, conifers, cycads (palm-like plants), and the similar benettitaleans. Ferns and horsetails covered the ground and bordered lakes and river banks. The sauropods fed on the soft plants of the lakes or on the delicate leaves on the high branches of the trees that surrounded more open countryside. They shared their habitat with *Stegosaurus* and its relative *Kentrosaurus*. These plated dinosaurs were also plant-eaters. *Stegosaurus* may have been able to control its body temperature using the plates that run along its back.

Reality Bites

Extract 1.10: 'It's Not Always the Greatest' by Judy Blume

In the extract below, Judy Blume, author of such books as *Blubber* and *Just as Long as We're Together*, responds to some of the letters sent to her by readers of her books. These particular letters deal with the experience of school, and Judy Blume explains how sometimes students can have a pretty hard time of it.

It's Not Always the Greatest

> Dear Judy,
> I'm having a bad time. Everything at school is going wrong.
> Tricia, age 10

In our family my brother is famous for having kicked his kindergarten teacher in the stomach. He never did learn to like school. Years later, when Larry was in kindergarten, he would roll around on the floor in the morning, clutching his stomach, hoping that he wouldn't have to face another day in the classroom. Having seen the results of being turned off by school at an early age through my brother, I was determined to find the cause of Larry's unhappiness. It took weeks to discover that, as Larry puts it now, he was failing cutting. It turned out that Larry was the only left-handed child in his kindergarten class and the blunt-edged scissors were designed for right-handed children. My aunt, an elementary school principal, saved the day by buying Larry a pair of left-handed scissors. Today we can laugh about that incident, but it was very serious at the time.

It's hard for me to write this section because I come from a family of teachers. I once asked my mother, 'If you could live your life over again would you do anything differently?' 'Yes,' she answered, 'I would be a teacher.' She raised me to be a teacher. I graduated from the School of Education at New York University, where I majored in early childhood education. But I never actually taught. I don't know if I would have been a good teacher or not. I don't know if I would have had the necessary patience and understanding.

Until I wrote the book *Blubber* I created classroom teachers who were, for the most part, kind and sensitive, which reflected my admiration for my aunt and uncle. I know how many dedicated classroom teachers there are. I hear from them every year. And when I was growing up I was lucky enough to have some of them myself. These teachers treat their students with respect. They understand that everything that happens outside the classroom affects their students' performance and behaviour within. They are sure enough of themselves and their abilities to talk calmly and openly with the kids and with their parents. They are able to welcome differences of opinion. But not all kids are lucky enough to be blessed with such teachers every year. That is reality. And that is what the letters in this section are about.

Dear Judy,

My son's first-grade teacher is especially cruel to the boys in her class. She pulls their hair, raps them on their heads with her ballpoint pen and humiliates them in front of the other children. My son says if he was not a good reader it would be even worse for him. The boys who have trouble reading get the brunt of their teacher's rage.

I have tried talking to the principal but he did not want to hear what I had to say and he never allows children to change classes. I have tried talking to the other parents in the neighbourhood but they are apathetic. I cannot afford private school tuition and I don't know what else to do. I feel powerless.

Elaine, adult

And that is exactly how most kids feel – powerless – especially when it comes to their lives in school. Going to school is a child's work. It is usually their first experience of interacting with the world on their own.

Dear Judy,

I am in sixth grade. My teacher says I am a complete airhead. She gives me sickeningly low marks. I feel that I have the potential and desire to really be something, maybe an author or a journalist. But my teacher says I wouldn't be dedicated to my work enough. I try my best to show her she is wrong, but nothing works. She will never like me or think that my work is any good. I hate how she calls on me when I don't raise my hand. But when I do, she acts like she doesn't see it.

Christine, age 11

Dear Judy,

My teacher is always doing her nails and cutting out coupons. If one person talks when we are supposed to be quiet, she yells at us and keeps us after school. She makes us write one hundred times, I will not talk out of turn. So this one time I got really mad and instead of writing that, I wrote her a letter about how it isn't fair to punish all of us every time. But you know what? She never read my letter. I know because I watched her through the window in our classroom door and she dumped all our papers in the trash can as soon as we were gone.

Miriam, age 10

My daughter, Randy, had a teacher like Miriam's. She would come home from school angry almost every day.

I approached the school principal but he told me Randy's teacher had years of experience, and he wasn't going to interfere with her methods. There was no way I could solve Randy's problem. All I could do was empathise and encourage her to talk about her feelings. I think it helped just to let her know I was on her side.

Extract 1.11: 'Growing Up and Your Feelings' by Susan Meredith

The following extract is from a book, *Understanding the Facts of Life*, aimed at a readership of children and young adults. Here the writer is seeking to explain the emotional changes that take place as a young person moves from being a child to becoming a teenager.

As you become physically and emotionally more mature, you become more independent and your relationships with the people around you also alter. Some people find these changes stressful at times.

It may help to remember that other people are experiencing the same thing, and that older people went through similar experiences at one time. The way you feel may also be affected by physical changes in your body, over which you have no control.

Identity
Thinking about what kind of person you are and about what you want to do and be in the future is an important part of growing up. It can feel lonely and confusing sometimes, coming to terms with your adult personality.

Moods
At times, you may feel moody and irritable without really knowing why. Changes in your body's hormone levels can be partly to blame for this. Things usually improve as you get used to your adult body and feelings.

Independence
As you grow up, you will probably want to take more responsibility for your own life and actions. This can sometimes cause conflict with your parents, who have to adjust to the idea that you are becoming more independent.

Friends

Most teenagers make close friends and some even fall in love. You may form a close group of friends but beware of feeling that you must always do what the rest of the group do, especially if you feel uncomfortable or unhappy about it.

Shyness

Many adolescents suffer from shyness. They lack confidence in their looks and personality. How much you suffer and how you cope depends on your individual character. Remember that others often feel shy even if they do not look it.

Extract 1.12: 'Mummy's Having a Baby' by Dr Richard Woolfson

The article below comes from a magazine, *Practical Parenting*, aimed at those who have, or are about to have, a young family. In this article the writer explains how a small child may react to the arrival of a baby brother or sister, and what some parents may need to think about.

MUMMY'S HAVING
A BABY

A new baby is exciting for everyone, but your older child may need a little help to adjust ...

Unfair as it might seem on parents with one child, many mums say they only feel they're a 'proper family' once they've had their second baby. And there's no doubt that the birth of a little brother or sister brings huge changes, not just to your life, but to your first-born's, too. It's not always easy to make room for someone else when you've been used to taking centre stage.

Naturally, you want your child to be excited and happy about the prospect of a new baby, but don't be surprised if he seems apprehensive, or even angry. It's natural to be anxious at the thought of sharing you with someone else.

Sibling rivalry

The origins of sibling rivalry usually lie in the first five years of life. Your first-born child can feel knocked off his perch by the arrival of the new baby – after all, before the birth he had you all to himself – and resentment and jealousy often start.

Psychological research shows that even second- and third-born children can feel resentment towards a new baby. Younger children are likely to experience jealousy, too, especially when they think that older brothers and sisters are allowed more freedom, later bedtimes or more new clothes.

When this form of jealousy exists, it results at best in verbal disagreements between your children as they shout and even scream at each other. (Of course, you may be delighted to discover your children have a trouble-free relationship.)

Extract 1.13: 'Making Choices' from 'The Myth of Maturity' by Terri Apter

The extract below comes from a book mainly aimed at advising the parents of teenage children. In this extract the author explains some of the difficulties that teenagers confront when they are on the brink of leaving home.

Former US President Harry Truman is reported to have said: 'I have found the best way to give advice to your children is to find out what they want and to advise them to do it.' Wise though this remark is, it overlooks one of the most difficult problems young people face as they become adults: All too often they simply do not yet know what they want to do. As young people feel pressured to make decisions about future courses and careers, they feel as though they are standing on a precipice and being commanded to fly. For many thresholders, and their parents, the greatest challenge is to answer the question, 'Where do I head for when I get going?'

In a society that provides so much freedom, so many opportunities – and so few charts and anchors – choosing a path (and therefore closing off other options) can be confusing. Those who are struck dumb by the prospect of making decisions need help managing the stress and risks of choice.

Those crucial decisions of the threshold years – what to study, where to live, which jobs to seek – are both necessary and tiresome. Growing up means being responsible for the choices we make, and this can be daunting. 'Maybe I won't like what I choose,' 'What if I mess up?' 'What if it's too hard?' they ask. The process of making choices can trigger high anxiety and low self-esteem as a thresholder assumes everyone around her has a better-planned future than she does. It can lead to an unsettling series of decisions, which are rapidly reformulated, as none seems to be the right one. Some young people describe being caught up in a useless spin of self-questioning where 'What do I want to do?' constantly echoes in their brain. They know that, in theory, opportunities are *out there*, but they do not know how to meet up with them.

Many thresholders feel paralysed as they confront their options. Some worry that they will make the wrong choice and end up doing what they do not enjoy or what they are not able to do well. They worry they will miss out on something by choosing one thing rather than another. 'Potentialitis' is the term used to describe the paralysis that strikes young people when they feel they must keep their options open at all costs lest they lose the glow of endless possibilities ahead of them. With new opportunities come anxieties: Am I making the right choices? Do I like this course, this club? Will I succeed in what I'm planning to do? What am I giving up, by choosing this rather than something else?

Some young people feel in conflict with what their parents want for them. Even though they say to themselves, 'The decision is up to me' or 'I don't care what my parents say', deep down they do care and feel trapped by what they know their parents would prefer. They may worry that a parent's hopes do not match theirs or that they have been so used to thinking along a parent's lines that they cannot yet formulate what they want.

Far more than a passing phase, an inability to make choices can put the brakes on development. Unable to identify their interests, unable to form goals or commit themselves to plans, many thresholders disengage from the entire process. They may become apathetic: 'I don't care what I do.' They may opt for simplistic optimism: 'Things will turn out OK'. Parents are stunned to see a once forward-planning daughter or son shy away from the task of shaping his or her own life. Just at the point at which they are expected to be independently motivated, they suffer a loss of all desire and direction. Puzzled and impatient, parents diagnose stubbornness, laziness, lack of backbone, or 'immaturity'. 'Why can't you make up your mind?' young people often report being asked. 'Isn't it time you settled on something? You have to make plans. You can't just drift. You have to have some direction in life.' These responses compound their problems: the people who might offer them guidance, instead 'badger' or 'judge' them.

The following conditions play a role in the special problems today's thresholders have in making choices:

1 Normal self-doubt and indecisiveness can be aggravated when thresholders are offered too much choice and too little guidance.
2 Parents' disappointment at a daughter's or son's indecisiveness leads to further anxiety and conflict.
3 High expectations of personal fulfilment make the limitations of any particular choice difficult to tolerate.

Parents need to educate themselves about the new worlds their sons and daughters move in. Modern trends and expectations are making choices much more difficult for this future generation of thresholders.

Writing to explain: Activities

Before reading – oral activities

1 **Oral activity for access:**

   a In a pair or in a small group, each in turn give a short explanation (maximum 2 minutes) of how you perform a simple domestic task (toasting a slice of bread, making a cup of tea, etc.).

   b The person (or people) listening should note down any question they would like to ask about anything that did not seem quite clear in the explanation.

   c Pool your questions and discuss what makes a good explanation (organisation? detail?).

2 **Oral activity for assessment (individual extended contribution – explain):**

   a On your own, note down the different subjects on the school curriculum.

   b Which subject do you think is the most important? Note down your reasons.

   c Prepare your talk on the most important subject in school so that it will be clear and interesting (and fun?). Explain the reasons for your choice in as much detail as possible.

   d Give your talk – and be prepared to answer questions.

During reading

As you read the extracts in this section, you need to be on the lookout for what it is the writer or writers are trying to explain and how they are going about it – what about graphics, layout, bullet-points, etc.? How long or short are their paragraphs, and the sentences within the paragraphs?

How much detail do they give, and how do they give it?

1 While you are reading, make notes on:

   a What the topic is that the writer is explaining.

   b How much detail they give.

   c The way they set out their explanation (both how the explanation is organised into paragraphs and how any graphics, charts etc. are used).

   d How they build up a relationship with the reader (humour, use of comparisons, etc.).

   e Does the text (or texts) succeed? Why? Are there any difficulties?

2 When you have finished reading, discuss your findings with a partner or in a small group. Pool your ideas and make a few brief notes on what, in your view, makes a good explanation.

After reading

Select a question from *either* the linked writing *or* the coursework questions at the end of this book and follow the instructions to help you prepare and answer the question.

Writing to describe

Extract 1.14: 'The Matron' by Roald Dahl

The passage below is an extract from Roald Dahl's autobiography *Boy*, in which he describes his early childhood. Here he paints a picture of the Matron at the boarding school he was sent to when he was seven, and the terror she aroused in the hearts of her young charges.

At St Peter's the ground floor was all classrooms. The first floor was all dormitories. On the dormitory floor the Matron ruled supreme. This was her territory. Hers was the only voice of authority up here, and even the eleven- and twelve-year-old boys were terrified of this female ogre, for she ruled with a rod of steel.

The Matron was a large fair-haired woman with a bosom. Her age was probably no more than twenty-eight but it made no difference whether she was twenty-eight or sixty-eight because to us a grown-up was a grown-up and all grown-ups were dangerous creatures at this school.

Once you had climbed to the top of the stairs and set foot on the dormitory floor, you were in the Matron's power, and the source of this power was the unseen but frightening figure of the Headmaster lurking down in the depths of his study below. At any time she liked, the Matron could send you down in your pyjamas and dressing-gown to report to this merciless giant, and whenever this happened you got caned on the spot. The Matron knew this and she relished the whole business.

She could move along that corridor like lightning, and when you least expected it, her head and her bosom would come popping through the dormitory doorway. 'Who threw that sponge?' the dreaded voice would call out. 'It was *you*, Perkins, was it not? Don't lie to me,

Perkins! Don't argue with me! I know perfectly well it was you! Now you can put your dressing-gown on and go downstairs and report to the Headmaster this instant!'

In slow motion and with immense reluctance, little Perkins, aged eight and a half, would get into his dressing-gown and slippers and disappear down the long corridor that led to the back stairs and the Headmaster's private quarters. And the Matron, as we all knew, would follow after him and stand at the top of the stairs listening with a funny look on her face for the *crack ... crack ... crack* of the cane that would soon be coming up from below. To me that noise always sounded as though the Headmaster was firing a pistol at the ceiling of his study.

Looking back on it now, there seems little doubt that the Matron disliked small boys very much indeed. She never smiled at us or said anything nice, and when for example the lint stuck to the cut on your kneecap, you were not allowed to take it off yourself bit by bit so that it didn't hurt. She would always whip it off with a flourish, muttering, 'Don't be such a ridiculous little baby!'

Extract 1.15: 'Far from Shore' by Robert Kunzig

This is an extract from the introduction to *Mapping the Deep: The extraordinary story of Ocean Science*, a book about life in and under the sea. Robert Kunzig conjures up a vivid picture of what you could see out of your bedroom window, if your bedroom happened to be deep on the ocean floor ...

Imagine you looked out your window one morning and saw jellyfish. Not just the occasional songbird fluttering or hawk circling, soon to alight again, but a sky full of floating gelatinous animals, jellyfish and ctenophores and salps sucking in microscopic plankton. Every now and then a shark or a tuna glides through noiselessly; every now and then one of the jellies starts glowing like a giant firefly. A sky like that would be worth exploring, would it not?

Imagine that when you picked up your newspaper, the lead story concerned a mountain range newly discovered in Switzerland. Its peaks, according to the paper, were higher than 10,000 feet; geographers were amazed. You would be amazed too, would you not?

Imagine, finally, that when you stepped out into your backyard, you discovered a new species of plant. And reporting this to the proper authorities, you learned that this plant of yours, which no one had seen before, because no one had looked, was so fabulously abundant in everybody's backyard that it seemed to be exerting a significant influence on the climate of the whole planet. Perhaps you can imagine that; perhaps not.

The ocean is a sky like that, a backyard like that. It is 320 million cubic miles of water covering 140 million square miles of seafloor covering seven-tenths of Earth. Great discoveries remain to be made there, discoveries as big as mountains – or as *Arcitheuthis*, the giant squid.

Giant squid are the world's largest invertebrate animals, as much as 60 feet long; we know that because from time to time their corpses wash ashore somewhere. But they have never been observed scientifically in their native habitat. In 1999 the Smithsonian Institution in Washington organised an expedition whose chief purpose was to find a giant squid in the waters off New Zealand, where fishermen have hauled up the odd *Arcitheuthis* in their nets. The researchers stayed for a month with their television crew, diving daily in a submersible, reporting their observations of whales and other creatures on the expedition website – but they never saw *Arcitheuthis*. Maybe by the time you read this someone will have. But maybe not. The ocean is still a place where giant squid, and much else, can still hide.

Extract 1.16: 'The Witch' by Amanda Vlietstra

The passage below is from an article in a magazine called *Spirit and Destiny*, which has a readership of those interested in the spiritual and the occult. Here the writer describes her encounter with Cassandra Latham, a professional witch.

The Witch

Cassandra Latham started having visions and seeing spirits at an early age, but she was in her thirties before she realised she was a witch!

'Although I was working as a nurse and therefore caring for people, I still had this unfulfilled gap in my life,' she says. 'I'd had an unhappy childhood, and I escaped into a fairytale world full of make-believe just to survive. I'd looked into many religions but none of them fitted the gut feeling I had. Then, one day, I met a couple at a friend's house who I later discovered were witches.

'The more I questioned them, the more they told me about witchcraft and paganism, and how it all fitted in with nature and respecting the world,' she continues. 'And suddenly it all slotted into place. My communing with nature, the growth cycle and my general philosophy. I remember the night it dawned on me. I walked home across the fields in a daze. Finally I made the connection.'

Cassandra started reading up on paganism and witchcraft, and met other witches. For a short time, she was a member of a coven, but soon realised she preferred the solitary life.

Then, ten years ago, a back injury forced Cassandra to give up nursing. Nowadays, she makes her living from Wicca, following in the age-old footsteps of the traditional village wise woman and performing blessings and weddings, and selling charms and spells. She's managed to do this with a little help from the goddess and, of course, her business start-up adviser.

'The chap running the business course was slightly stunned when I told him about my chosen profession,' she laughs. 'But then he recovered and said it was going to be interesting. We realised that what I do fits in perfectly with business management. I do marketing, deal with customers and deliver a good service. I needed to brush up on my website skills but in the four years I have been a professional witch I've never been overdrawn and business is good.'

But it's not just about money, of course. 'When I was asked to take on the unpaid position as Minister at the Royal Cornwall Hospitals NHS Trust six years ago, I was very pleased. As a nurse, I already knew the value of understanding and positive energy.

'I could be there just to offer comfort to a patient, or it could be to administer the last rites. The life force and energy of the spirit as it moves on is wonderful, and I don't find it depressing – it's an immense privilege.

'People can be helped simply by listening to them and laying their problems before them in an easy-to-understand way ... As a witch, I can cast a spell to speed up that process, but the end result is still the same as listening and empowering others.'

Extract 1.17: 'Into the Lion's Den' by Matthew Weiner

The extract below is from an article in which Matthew Weiner, a Jewish journalist, describes how he went undercover to investigate the youth wing of the British National Party. It was not an altogether serene experience ...

Paintballing, drinking beer and sitting round a camp fire fuelled by Anti-Nazi League posters. Jewish journalist Matthew Weiner spends a day at a British National Party youth camp.

Ask anyone who's been to summer camp as a child and they'll tell you the first day is definitely the worst. They'll probably recall how on the journey to the campsite they desperately wanted to turn around and that they've rarely felt such jitters since.

Aged 28, I should have left those feelings well behind me. But as a Jew travelling up to Camp Excalibur, the British National Party's youth camp, they all came flooding back. According to my religion's law I should be in synagogue this morning, observing the Sabbath. I shouldn't be driving and I definitely shouldn't be heading up the M1 towards a field near Bradford to break bread with a gaggle of far-right activists, some of whom deny the Holocaust ever happened.

Whitney Houston once sang that she believed the children are our future. She wasn't alone; the BNP entirely agree. That's why for the last two years Mark Collett, referred to as a 'rough diamond' by party leader Nick Griffin, has been running Camp Excalibur for white youths aged 18 to 24. Naturally, worrying parallels have been drawn between this event and the Hitler Youth. As far as the crew-cut Collett is concerned, however, the unflattering comparison is all that can be expected from a mainstream media that is, according to him, 'controlled by Zionists'.

Ever since the Cambridge University-educated Griffin wrestled the helm of the BNP from John Tyndall in 1999, his aim has been to turn the rag-tag association of racists, nationalists and Nazi sympathisers into what he considers to be a respectable political party. By all accounts he's done rather well. Collett, a business economics graduate from Leeds University (despite attempts by the Anti-Nazi League to have him thrown out) is rumoured to be dating Griffin's daughter. He is also considered to be a chip off her father's block and a hot prospect for the emerging party's future.

Picking him out from the crowd of skinheads milling about at Camp Excalibur is pretty easy – his voice is the loudest. Clutching the crate of Carling he has asked me to bring, I approach him. 'You're not as weaselly-looking as I thought you would be,' he says, to the amusement of his cohorts. 'That's a compliment, y'know.' I smile weakly: 'Thanks.'

Collett is collecting subs from everyone who has just arrived at the site – about £80 in all. For the very reasonable price of £10 per person, the Young BNPs will be treated to a weekend of outdoor activities including paintball, canoeing and five-a-side football. All good, wholesome fun.

The campsite stands high up in the hills of Queensbury, with a sweeping vista of Bradford down below. Bathed in the late-September sun, shaven-headed kids run after a pug-faced dog while their mum, wearing a Union Jack flag as a sarong, puts up the tent with her husband. Small groups of teenagers in combat clothes chat while politely queueing to hand over their subs. As one proud father (Mr White) clutching a toddler (White junior) hands over his tenner, Collett says: 'That's the Whites paid for.' Then, realising his pun, he adds, 'and that's exactly what we like to see at a BNP event!' Everyone laughs. I pay my contribution, wincing inwardly as I imagine it winging its way to the BNP coffers.

Paintballing with political extremists is a less than savoury experience. Maybe it's the fascist overtones of the skinheads and army fatigues that make this harmless activity seem rather more ominous, or perhaps it's the fact that one of our number, Nick Griffin's right-hand man Tony Lecomber, is a convicted nail-bomb terrorist.

We start off with a quick game called Capture the Flag in which two teams compete to rescue the Union Jack and return it to their base. The first round is easily won by Collett's team. 'The key to paintball,' says the victor to an audience of keen youngsters as he reloads the pump-action rifles, 'is not to fanny around in your base, but to come out and do something. That is also the philosophy of the BNP,' he adds.

Soon it is my team's turn to face Collett's and I find myself guarding our base. The game starts with a flurry of activity. Suddenly, from the thick of the mêlée, the leader of the Young BNP emerges from behind a hillock to confront me. Locked in combat, we rattle off countless rounds at each other until one of my paint pellets finds its mark, splattering his chin with fluorescent yellow paint. Despite accusations of 'cheat!' from those watching on the sidelines, he ignores the hit and goes on to win the game for his side. Rules are not going to get in the way of Collett's desperately ambitious bid for victory.

Later on, back at the campsite, while everyone is warming themselves in front of a bonfire fuelled by Anti-Nazi League leaflets and banners, Collett's tongue has been loosened thanks to a couple of my Carlings. 'Martin Luther King had a dream,' I say to him, 'that one day black and white children might get along like sisters and brothers ...'

'Martin Luther King didn't have any dreams,' spits Collett in retort. 'He was no great man: he was a communist agitator who repeatedly slept with whores. I have a dream,' he says, finding his rhythm. 'I have a dream of seeing a healthy white British Britain. I have a dream of putting the "Great" back into Britain. That's my dream.'

It's going to take a lot more than a paintball to stop Mark Collett.

Extract 1.18: 'The Girl in the Red Dress' by Thomas Keneally

In *Schindler's Ark*, later filmed by Steven Spielberg as *Schindler's List*, Australian writer Thomas Keneally described the true story of Oskar Schindler, a German industrialist without any apparent beliefs other than in his own pleasure, who somehow felt drawn to risk his own life to save the lives of thousands of Jews right under the nose of the Nazi regime during the Second World War. This extract shows the moment when the true horror of what was happening to the Jews was first forced on Oskar's attention.

South of the ghetto, beyond Rekawka Street, rose a hilly parkland. There was an intimacy, like that of medieval siege paintings, about the way you could look down over the ghetto's southern wall. As you rode along the brow of the hills the ghetto's map was revealed, and you could see, as you passed them, what was happening in the streets below.

Schindler had noticed this advantage while riding here with Ingrid in the spring. Now he decided to go riding again. He hired horses from the stables in Bednarskiego Park. They were impeccably turned out, he and Ingrid, in long hacking jackets, riding britches and dazzling boots. Two Sudetan blonds high above the disturbed antheap of the ghetto.

They rode up through the woods and had a short gallop over open meadows. From their saddles they could now see Wegierska Street. Schindler noticed that in Wegierska Street two lines were continually forming. One was stable, but the other, as it lengthened, was regularly marched away in sections around the corner into Józefínska and out of sight. It was not hard to interpret this assembling and movement, since Schindler and Ingrid, fringed by pine trees and elevated above the ghetto, were a distance of only two or three short blocks from the action.

As families were routed out of the apartments, they were separated forcibly into two lines without regard for family consideration. Adolescent daughters with the proper papers went to the static line, from which they called out to their middle-aged mothers in the other. A nightshift worker, still sullen from disturbed sleep, was pointed to one line, his wife and child to the other.

Oskar and Ingrid wheeled their horses, crossed a deserted avenue and, after a few metres, rode out on to a limestone platform facing directly down Krakusa.

In its closer reaches, this street was not as hectic as Wegierska. A line of women and children, not so long, was being led away towards Piwna Street. A guard walked in front, another strolled behind. There was an imbalance in the line: far more children than the few women in it themselves could have borne. At the rear, dawdling, was a toddler, boy or girl, dressed in a small scarlet coat and cap. It compelled Schindler's interest.

Schindler consulted Ingrid. It was definitely a girl, said Ingrid. Little girls got obsessed by colour, especially a bright colour like that.

As they watched, the Waffen SS man at the rear of the column would occasionally put out his hand and correct the drift of this scarlet node. He did not do it harshly – he could have been an elder brother. Had he been asked by his officers to do something to allay the sentimental concern of watching civilians, he could not have done better. So the moral anxiety of the two riders in Badnarskiego Park was, for an impulsive second, irrationally allayed. But it was brief comfort. For behind the departing column of women and children, to which the scarlet toddler placed a meandering full stop, SS teams with dogs worked north along either side of the street.

They rampaged through the fetid apartments – as a symptom of their rush, a suitcase flew from a second storey window and split open on the pavement. And, running before the dogs, the men and women and children who had hidden in attics or cupboards, inside drawerless dressers, the evaders of the first wave of search, jolted out into the pavement, yelling and gasping in terror of the Dobermanns. Everything seemed speeded-up, difficult for the viewers on the hill to keep pace with. Those who had emerged were shot where they stood on the pavement, flying out over the gutters from the impact of the bullets, gushing blood into the drains. A mother and a boy, perhaps eight, perhaps a scrawny ten, had retreated under a windowsill on the western side of Krakusa Street.

[Schindler's] eyes slewed up Krakusa Street to the scarlet child. They were doing it within half a block of *her*: they hadn't waited for her column to turn out of sight into Józefíñska. Schindler could not have explained at first how that compounded the murders on the pavement. Yet somehow it proved, in a way no one could ignore, their serious intent. While the scarlet child stopped in her column and turned to watch, they shot the woman beneath the windowsill in the neck, and one of them, when the boy slid down the wall whimpering, jammed a boot down on his head as if to hold it still and put the barrel against the back of the neck – the recommended SS target – and fired.

Oskar looked again for the small red girl. She had stopped and turned and seen the boot descend. A gap had already widened between her and the next last in the column. Again the SS guard fraternally corrected her drift, nudged her back into line. Herr Schindler could not see why he did not bludgeon her with his rifle butt, since at the other end of Krakusa Street mercy had been cancelled.

Extract 1.19: 'Jade Eyes' by Adrian Levy and Cathy Scott-Clark

The extract below is taken from a book by two journalists tracing the history of imperial green jade from ancient times to the present day. This soft green stone has been mined for thousands of years, and is much prized for its rarity and beauty. In order to visit the mines in Myanmar (Burma) where the jade is still being mined today, Adrian Levy and Cathy Scott-Clark had to pose as mining engineers to get past the military dictatorship's security system. This is a description of part of what they found.

The market ended where the evil-smelling Uru River ran through town, bobbing with empty penicillin bottles, the razor-sharp remains of severed Coca-Cola cans nestling in a log-jam of charred silver-foil. The orange ribbon of sewage, in which women beat their clothes against boulders, had been re-routed on the orders of armed forces chief, General Maung Aye's son-in-law, to expose a jadeite vein, the Corporal said, and before us was all that remained of the Kachin Hills. The once verdant peaks and tangled slopes had been sculpted into thin chimneys of rock and earth, whittled away by years of hard labour. Below, the valley floor plunged into an amber chasm that appeared to engulf everything in its path. Its walls, like a Roman amphitheatre, dropped hundreds of feet into the dark, where only the fluttering shadows of miners could be seen amid the dust. As we drew nearer we could make out thousands of nearly naked men and women cloaked in mud and bamboo hats, hauling boulders and earth in cane baskets. Others plunged eight-foot steel staves into the hillside, breaking away crumbs of rock and soil. To the left, men and women washed themselves in the slurry, pouring it over their heads and limbs. To the right, skeletal wooden ladders rose out of the crater and ran up rock chimneys. The miners who scaled them, those who scrambled along the sharply winding hairpin paths, the distant figures chipping away in the chasm and on top of the hills, the cantilevered gantries that whirred as they hauled rocks up to the surface, all moved in unison like the workings of a giant glass-backed watch, with its springs and balances, spinning-cogs and wheels driven in precision by jewels.

The heat forced us back, and we squatted in the shade of a tipper truck until a flood of people overflowed from the lip of the cauldron, spilling past us with down-turned faces, all registered by a young woman who checked their names against a human inventory. Saturated with sweat, blistered and panting, they threw their loads into the waiting trucks, oblivious to everything, conscious only of the long climb back down into the fiery pit.

All we had with us was a small instant camera, afraid that anything more sophisticated would not pass for the tools of a mining consultant interested in the process of extraction rather than the human by-product. For the first time we attempted to grab some pictures and forced our way to the edge of the pit. The people straining under the weight of their soil-packed panniers parted without losing a stride. There was no talk, no curious smiles or outstretched arms, only a dogged determination to reach the trucks and the end of the shift.

Of course, the Corporal saw us with our camera and charged over. We thought of trying to cover it with our shirts but he was on us in seconds. 'You'll get a better view of it all if you come round here,' he said, and, to our amazement, took us behind a gantry. 'You want to take a closer look, to see how we do it?' He dodged between the ascending miners and we followed him down, gasping for air, the dust choking our throats and eyes, until we reached the very bottom, coated in a moist yellow film that was glazed by the incendiary air. Hundreds of diggers and carriers, all lacquered with mud, turned to look at us. Suddenly a miner dropped to his knees, his bruised arms scooping a stone out of the dirt, but the Corporal was there before him. 'Green, green. I saw it first,' he yelled, knocking the teenage digger aside, snatching his splinter of jadeite. The boy fell to the ground, his longyi riding up, his spindly legs and arms a jumble of bamboo poles. 'A present from Hpakant,' the Corporal said, presenting us with the nugget. We were too ashamed to look at the miner who had lost his shard of jadeite and walked away, crawling up the hairpins and out of the chasm. We had had enough of the Corporal for one day, but he lagged behind us, eyes trained on the spoil. He appeared to find it hard to leave the money pit that intoxicated everybody who climbed into it. 'Jade eyes,' he said, catching us up, gasping for air. 'I have jade eyes.'

Extract 1.20: 'A Chronicle of Love' by Vera Brittain

At the beginning of the First World War, Vera Brittain was just 21. Throughout the war, she kept a detailed diary of her experiences and feelings. One of the experiences she describes is that of a deeply-felt love affair with a young man called Roland Leighton, a schoolfriend of her brother's. The extracts below describe how the affair began, and how it ended.

1914

Wednesday December 30th, London

This has been a day of surprising realisations and developments — half ecstatic, wholly turbulent. I travelled down with Edward by the 9.50; Mother and Daddy said goodbye to him quite cheerfully, which was more than I expected. We met Aunt Belle by the Charing Cross left-luggage office. She hadn't changed a scrap since I last saw her, nor did she make any observation on the alteration of my appearance, though I was not grown up when she last saw me. We met Roland at the Comedy Restaurant and had lunch. It seemed perfectly natural to see Roland in khaki, I suppose because I saw him in the Corps at Uppingham. We were perfectly incapable of saying anything to each other during lunch.

Then I found myself in a whirl of the most surprising proportions — I had mentioned during lunch, quite without thinking, that I wanted to see David Copperfield, and nothing would satisfy him but that he should take us tomorrow evening. I demurred at first but Aunt Belle — who of course would have to chaperon me — was quite ready to go and finally I consented.

Thursday December 31st

The old year departs in a whirl of the deepest and most conflicting emotions I have ever known, a tumult of love and sorrow. I went up to London to begin my shopping in a state of weariness and confused sentiments, since I scarcely slept at all last night, partly because I was thinking about Roland and wondering just what I really did feel.

At lunch time Roland arrived outside D. H. Evans, where we had promised to meet him, in a taxi, and put us into it and drove off to the Florence Restaurant for lunch. In the taxi he gave me a lovely bunch of violets, sweet-smelling and fresh. He was a little perturbed because he had not brought Aunt Belle any flowers, but she smoothed him down most tactfully and then remarked 'My dear lad, you can't be expected to have two people in your head at once!'

At last the delightful party broke up, for I had to go to the tailor's. When we had finished Roland was waiting for us — again with a taxi — outside, and handed Aunt Belle some pale pink carnations, and me a glorious bunch of pink roses, all covered with dew and of so sweet a scent that their perfume seemed to cling to me like a benediction the whole evening.

We had a warm, secluded corner at dinner just below the balcony. The table was round, and Roland sat opposite to me; I found it much easier to talk to him there than when he sat beside me. We started on a conversation which would have seemed extraordinary to any of the other people in the restaurant could they have heard it; we were discussing how we should best like to be buried. The discussion grew more and more melancholy, though we were quite unsentimental over it, till finally I asked Roland whether he would like to be killed in action. Aunt Belle said 'My dear girl, why do you talk about such things?' but he answered quite quietly 'Yes, I should; I don't want to die, but if I must, I should like to die that way. Anyhow, I should hate to go right through this war without being wounded at all; I should want something to prove that I had been in action.' I sat looking at him with his expressive dark eyes and broad strong figure and suddenly was conscious of a deep sense of tragedy in my heart both for my sake and his; for mine because I love him and for his because it seems the greatest crime in the world that so brilliant an intellect and so promising a character should soon be exposed to danger and death.

His Majesty's Theatre is quite near the Florence, so we walked to it and arrived in excellent time. As the evening wore on I thought less and less about the play and more and more of his nearness to me. Everything these two days had been dreamlike and incomplete; almost everything we could have said to each other had been left unsaid, but I knew the one thing that made all the difference in the world — that the feelings which, ever since I had known him I had thought might quite possibly arise between us, were no longer a dream but a reality.

The most precious evening of my life thus far was over at last.

1915

Monday December 27th

I had just finished dressing when a message came to say that there was a telephone message for me. I sprang up joyfully, thinking to hear in a moment the dear dreamed-of tones of the beloved voice.

But the telephone message was not from Roland but from Clare; it was not to say that Roland had arrived, but that instead had come this telegram:

T 223. Regret to inform you that Lieut. R.A. Leighton 7th Worcesters died of wounds December 23rd. Lord Kitchener sends his sympathy.
Colonel of Territorial Force, Records, Warwick.

New Year's Eve 11.55

This time last year He was seeing me off on Charing Cross Station after David Copperfield – and I had just begun to realise I loved Him. Today He is lying in the military cemetery at Louvencourt – because a week ago He was wounded in action, and had just 24 hours of consciousness more and then went 'to sleep in France'. And I, who in impatience felt a fortnight ago that I could not wait another minute to see Him, must wait till all Eternity. All has been given me, and all taken away again – in one year.

Writing to describe: Activities

Before reading – oral activities

1 **Oral activity for access:**

   When you are describing something, you are trying to give your reader a picture of what something or somebody was like, or an idea of a particular feeling or emotion.

   a On your own or in a small group, note down very brief descriptions of your school – one to make it sound the most attractive place in the world, the kind of place that people would want to go to for their holidays, and another to make it sound the worst possible place anyone could imagine.

   b Share your descriptions with each other.

   c Spend a short time picking out the words and phrases that gave your listener different pictures and emotions (for example, adjectives, adverbs, a range of different verbs, different word order for emphasis).

2 **Oral activity for assessment (individual extended contribution – describe):**

   a On your own, choose a place which you like (perhaps somewhere you have been to on holiday, or somewhere you go to have fun – a gym, a dance studio, somewhere you go fishing, etc.) or a person who you care about (for example, a friend, a cousin, a grandparent).

   b Brainstorm everything that you know about this place or person, noting down particularly what this place or person looks like and what you enjoy about them.

   c Arrange your ideas so that your listeners will get a clear picture of this place or person, trying to use words that will make your listeners feel as positive about them as you do.

d Describe your chosen place or person to the class as a whole, so that they can picture them in their mind's eye and feel as warmly towards them as you do.

During reading

1 As you read the extracts in this section, look out for all the different techniques used to make what is being described come alive for the reader, whether it is a place, a person or an experience.

2 a When you have finished reading, select a passage or paragraph that seemed to you particularly effective and make brief notes of anything that struck you about the writer's technique – for instance, their use of verbs and adverbs, their use of adjectives, the way they used metaphors or similes, how they organised the material to build up an atmosphere and keep the reader interested.

b Share your notes with a partner or in a small group, and write a short paragraph beginning '*To write a good description that comes alive for the reader you need to...*'. You may like to use short references or quotations from the extract or extracts you have studied.

After reading

Select a question from *either* the linked writing *or* the coursework questions at the end of this book and follow the instructions to help you prepare and answer the question.

Section 2

Writing to analyse, review, comment

Whether you are analysing something, reviewing it or commenting on it, you are writing from a point of view which suggests both an interest in the topic and an opinion about it. At the very least, an analysis suggests an interest in the topic and a desire to find out about it, while both review and comment suggest that you have an opinion on the subject which you want to share with others. The paragraphs below may help you clarify your ideas about these different kinds of writing.

Writing to analyse: All the passages in this section are concerned with analysing something – an event, an experience, a process. Writing to analyse suggests a certain authority on the part of the writer, and a certain inquisitiveness: What has happened? Why has it happened? In this section you will read an analysis of why some penguins are finding life hard in Antarctica, what the thinking was behind the writing of the film *Welcome to Sarajevo*, how some aspects of family life work, and much more.

Writing to review: All the texts in this section are reviews – that is to say, a discussion or an analysis in which the writer gives their *opinion* of the topic they are dealing with. Here reviewers give their views on different kinds of books, on films and on advertising campaigns.

Writing to comment: All of the writers of the texts in this section are commenting on something – that is, describing an event, idea or experience with some degree of personal involvement. They are not trying to argue a point of view, or persuade their readers to some course of action – rather they are saying, this is what I found or experienced, and here are some thoughts I had about it.

Writing to analyse

Extract 2.1: 'Being 100 per cent sure' by Barbara de Angelis

The extract below is taken from a book entitled *The 100 Most Asked Questions about Sex, Love and Relationships*. Here Barbara de Angelis is looking at the question of what makes a relationship work.

Can you ever be 100 per cent sure that someone you're with is the right one for you? What qualities should you look for in a partner?

I don't know about 100 per cent – nothing in life is certain, because everything is constantly changing. However, I do believe strongly that if you learn as much as you can about love, intimacy and compatibility, you can be very sure that you have chosen the right partner. And here's a very important lesson about compatibility, one that has changed my life: *The key to choosing the right partner is to look for a person with good character, not simply a good personality.*

Most of us become initially attracted to a mate because of something about his or her personality, or as your question mentioned, 'qualities' – his ability to make you laugh; her softness; his interest in cycling, etc. While these traits might be enjoyable, they aren't what's going to determine whether or not this relationship makes you truly happy. For that, you have to look for character. **Character determines how a person will treat himself, you, and, one day, your children. It is the foundation of any healthy partnership**. If you think of a relationship as a cake, personality is like the icing, but character is the substance.

It's not enough to ask yourself the question: *Does my partner love me?* You need to ask a much more important question: *How capable is my partner of loving, period?* I've found there are six areas you can look at in a potential partner that define his or her character, and that will help you answer this question and determine how ready this person is to be in a committed relationship.

1 Commitment to personal growth

I've listed this characteristic first because I feel it is one of the most important traits to seek in a partner. If you find someone who is committed to their personal growth, you will already have avoided many of the problems couples face: one person wants to work on the relationship and the other doesn't; one partner tries to talk about the issues and the other refuses; one person sees areas that need improvement and the other is in denial.

2 Emotional openness

An intimate relationship is not based on sharing a home, a bed, or bathroom. It's based on sharing *feelings*. That's why the second quality you should look for in a partner is emotional openness. This means your mate:

a has feelings
b knows *what* he is feeling
c chooses to *share* those feelings with you
d knows *how* to express those feelings to you.

I can't tell you how many excuses I've heard from men and women in unhappy relationships about why their partner can't express feelings: **If your partner cannot identify and share his feelings with you, he is not ready to be in an intimate relationship.**

3 Integrity

Honesty, integrity, and trustworthiness are essential ingredients for a healthy relationship. Knowing that you can count on your partner to be truthful with you at all times will give you a tremendous sense of security. Finding a partner who has integrity means seeking:

- *Someone who is honest with himself.* There are many people who don't lie to you, but lie to themselves. Honesty begins at home, so to speak. *That means you should avoid mates who are masters of self-deception.*
- *Someone who is honest with others.* Does your partner lie to his clients or associates, all in the name of 'business'? Does your girlfriend hide the truth about her life from her family? Does your mate often justify doing things at work you feel lack integrity? *If you doubt your partner's integrity, you will lose respect for him,* and it will be difficult for you to trust his behaviour towards you.
- *Someone who is honest with you.* That means he will not hide parts of his life or personality from you; he won't tell you only what you want to hear in order to protect himself; he will share the truth with you without your having to trick him into admitting it, or pry it out of him.
- *Someone who doesn't play games.* Games belong on the playground, not in relationships.

4 Maturity and responsibility

Here are some signs that your partner is mature enough to have a relationship:

- *He (or she) can take care of him/herself.* If your partner has grown up sufficiently, he'll be able to earn enough money to support himself; know how to keep his living space relatively clean; know how to feed himself.
- *He is responsible. Responsibility means doing what you say you are going to do.* It means remembering to

pay the bills, keeping your promises, showing up on time, and not letting people down. It isn't a concept – it's an action.

• *He is respectful.*

5 High self-esteem

You've probably heard it said before, but it is true: **Your partner can only love you as much as he loves himself.** One of the biggest mistakes we make in choosing partners is focusing on how much our mate loves and treats us, and not how he treats himself. The healthier your partner's sense of self-esteem, the stronger your relationship will be.

6 Positive attitude toward life

There is an old saying that goes: *'There are two kinds of people in the world – positive people and negative people.'* If you had to spend the rest of your life with one of these kinds, which would you choose? Negative people always focus on problems, find something to complain about, allow worry to rule them, and are cynical. Someone with a positive attitude turns obstacles into opportunities, believes that things can always get better, and focuses on finding solutions.

Extract 2.2: 'Et in Arcadia Video' by Ken Hollings

This extract comes from the music magazine *The Wire*. In it the writer looks at the relationship between the growth of video arcade games and the use of music to enhance the 'real time' experience.

By camouflaging the process and programming lurking beneath every videogame simulation, music has become a crucial component of a 20 billion dollar industry. Ken Hollings uncovers how the true sound of the suburbs has twisted 'reality' to foster both the perfect killing machine and a generation of Otaku who prefer the certainties of the machine to the hazards of human interaction.

Illusion is experience accelerated. Simulation can only take place in real time. Play against a slow machine, one that takes several hours over each move, and you do not confront it directly. You know you're dealing with a process, a series of choices selected mechanically from a behavioural list. Everything changes as soon as the machine starts playing as fast as, if not faster than, a human. At this point you have no option but to take the machine on as a real opponent. You must attribute beliefs and ambitions to it or you lose the game. To use the technical term, the machine obliges its players to adopt the 'intentional stance', allowing them to make predictions about its future behaviour. In short, it replaces progression with narrative.

Like music, the videogame has a curious way of reflecting history as a complex spin of cultural factors.

Both industries have allowed technology and twitching, youthful energy to grapple freely with one another, creating whole empires out of loose change and percentage points in the process. Behind such fortunes lurk the usual moral panics. As with the early days of rock 'n' roll, videogames have long been accused of churning out a generation of cretinous, anarchistic goons, encouraging violent antisocial behaviour and hastening the decline of Western civilisation. Pay for play, however, has always remained a sound social concept. Thanks to a continuous stream of kids obediently shoving coins into slots just to be assaulted by strange lights and unearthly sounds, in a little over three decades the videogame has risen from being the record industry's hormonal younger brother to its biggest rival, boasting an annual global turnover to the north of 20 billion dollars. Music's relationship to videogaming is consequently anything but straightforward. There are brief moments of contact, dispersal and submersion, none of which are capable of forming themselves into neat lines of progress. In order to keep the game's interactive illusion in real time, music often blends so perfectly into the background that it virtually ceases to exist.

And yet it is always there. From the moment back in 1962 when the PDP-1 computer system's tape reader connected with the program for *Space War*, the first game ever written for a vectored screen, the organised reproduction of sound has maintained a powerful presence. It helped move computers out of the computer room, at a time when monsters like the PDP-1 effectively were the room, directly into social space. Produced in 1971 and debuting in what would become Silicon Valley, Nolan Bushnell's aptly named *Computer*

Space was the earliest commercially accessible arcade game. Combining *Space War*'s basic play with a sleek futuristic cabinet design, it established what would become the essential architecture of the videogame: a monitor, circuit board, control panel, loudspeaker and power supply. Throughout the 1970s, electronic sounds reproduced by loudspeaker helped introduce basic machine language into daily life and the home. The handheld range of games from Mattell Electronics made a big feature of their inbuilt speakers, as would such interactive diversions as Simon and Speak & Spell. Pretty soon, even the pocket calculator was busily drawing attention to itself through a high-pitched series of bleeps and trills. The addition of sound made the possibilities of interaction aggressively real. It marked a radical shift from the instant, a sixties concept that was already ageing badly, towards the immediate, which was about as 'now' as you could get. And if it felt like public space was being invaded by alien perceptions and attitudes, that's probably because it was.

Extract 2.3: 'Making *Welcome to Sarajevo*' by Frank Cottrell Boyce

This passage comes from the introduction to the screenplay of the film *Welcome to Sarajevo*. In his introduction the writer analyses the thought processes which led him to construct the film in the way that he did.

Opposite the block of flats in which I was born, there was a vast meadow of rubble which had been made, twenty years earlier, by a bomb dropped during the May Blitz. I grew up with the feeling I had missed the Big Event. The War was over, and there would never be another one. Not in Europe. I pestered my parents for tales of evacuation and air raids. I built squadrons of Airfix Spitfires. I never went anywhere without my arms stretched out like wings, making engine noises. If there was a war, I would be ready for it. Then a war did start in Europe and somehow I barely noticed. I was busy raising children, making a living, watching the O. J. Simpson trial. I knew people who were interested – a man from our parish collected a Luton van full of tinned food and drove it to Vukovar himself; an ex-boyfriend of my sister went to Croatia to take photographs. But when Graham Broadbent asked me if I wanted to write a film about Sarajevo, I said yes because I needed the money and because I wanted to work with Michael Winterbottom again, not because I had any strong feelings about it.

I began by watching tapes. I saw the amazing films made by SAGA in Sarajevo suring the siege. I watched Martin Bell's *Forcing the Peace*, and Michael Nicholson's passionate reports from the Ljubica Ivezic orphanage. Scenes of horror and heroism unfolded across the screen – lines of refugees, people queuing for water under sniper fire. Why had I been so apathetic about this? How had I allowed it to slip by me? Then I saw a tape by John Sweeney about the killing of a British photographer in Croatia. When they showed his face I reached for the freeze frame. That was him. Paul Jenks. My sister's ex. He was dead and I didn't even know. I rang my sister and she hadn't known either. It was then that the invisibility of the war really came home to me.

I'm not a journalist. I wasn't in Sarajevo during the siege. There were lots of things I didn't know. But I did know this one big fact – that this war had been ignored. I knew because I had ignored it.

Nothing I knew about screenwriting was any use to me when I was working on *Welcome to Sarajevo*.

Graham had bought the rights to Michael Nicholson's book *Natasha's Story* – an account of how Nicholson had met and finally adopted an orphan girl in Sarajevo during the siege. To begin with, this bothered me. I had seen enough films about Western journalists in faraway wars, struggling with their consciences and bosses while nameless natives got napalmed somewhere up country. When I read the book I felt differently. Nicholson had rescued one child. It was an act of moral heroism – a human gesture in an inhuman situation – but it wasn't epic. He was not Gladys Aylward, leading hundreds of children through enemy territory in *The Inn of the Sixth Happiness*. He had not unmasked a CIA conspiracy or smuggled secrets. It was moving and admirable, but also very simple. I could tell this story and still have room for other stories. I could use Nicholson as a starting point, then open out and tell the story of the siege itself – the daily grind of collecting firewood, scoring tobacco, wishing for soap, longing for something to happen. I could write a script that had some of the power of the SAGA films but was also accessible to a wider audience.

Reality Bites

The Nicholson character would be an Everyman, guiding us through the city. He would be based not on Nicholson himself but on Anybody. I wouldn't even go and meet Nicholson. It sounded really convincing when I pitched it and I got the job.

I thought it would be easy. I had a thousand great stories. Stories about how the people of Sarajevo had tried heroically to keep their city functioning and civilised while being pounded by two million Serb shells. There was the Sarajevo FC Football team, whose pitch became a mass grave; the Miss Sarajevo contest; the 'Beyond the End of the World' film festival held in the Radnik cinema on Snipers' Alley, when people ran a gauntlet of gunfire to get to the movies and so on. There was no shortage of heroes. There was Youssef Hajir – a refugee from Syria who opened the trauma hospital in Dobrinja in July 1992 and never lost a single patient to infection. There was Vedran Smiljovic who organised musicians everywhere to play Albinoni's *Adagio for Strings* at midday on the day the UN Council of Ministers came to visit. And of course there was Mrs Zoric, the Serb woman who ran the Ljubica Ivezic orphanage within sight of the Serb artillery, and who appears in the film as Mrs Savic.

I thought it would be easy because I had never written an Everyman character. Everyman characters are a swine. If Nicholson was to be the lens through which we looked at Sarajevo, then he had to be transparent. I'd spent years learning to push and explore characters. Now I had to write one that you would barely notice. All the interesting questions about Nicholson – like what made him pick Natasha, what his wife and other children thought of it, and so on – had to be closed down. It wasn't enough not to raise them; I had to make sure the audience didn't raise them either. They had to feel that it was the least he could have done, that they would have done the same.

Henderson had to be a character with no 'character arc'. He had to go to Sarajevo, do his things, and then carry on. In these times, when every adventure is played as therapy ('Yes, I did save the World from invading aliens, but more importantly, I discovered some important truths about my relationship with my father') the idea of a man just taking things in his stride was a kind of movie heresy.

The second problem was structure. Everyone is an expert in movie structure now. Everyone knows that films have three acts and that all the art is in the subtlety of the set-up and the aptness of the pay-off. However, Michael Winterbottom and I agreed that the film would only get the urgency it needed if we stuck as closely as possible to the facts. But facts are not like drama. In drama, characters make decisions, create their own fate and live with the consequences. In life, things happen by coincidence and chance. People set things up that don't pay off. They find themselves in the middle of situations before the exposition. Important characters vanish unexpectedly from their lives. Business is left unfinished and we are somehow never quite on stage for the big finale.

I tried at first to get the story into the traditional form, to put Henderson in control. I had him meeting Emira in the street more or less at the opening of the film. I made him seek her out. I made it harder for him to get Emira out of Sarajevo. But it took up too much space and it wasn't true. The fact is that Nicholson just happened to bump into someone who could help him one night in the Holiday Inn.

So I went the other way. I tried to write a screenplay in which the sequence seemed as random as war, in which the audience would never quite be sure where the next scene was coming from. I deliberately left Henderson's first meeting with Emira as late as I could. I put other children – the altar boy, the girl in the hospital – in the film to show that there was nothing special about Emira. I tried to get in as many scenes without Henderson as possible. I followed minor characters back to their homes. I had a five-minute section in the middle of the film about Arkan, the leading exponent of Ethnic Cleansing, in which none of our characters appeared. I added a section about the discovery of the concentration camps at Manjaca and Omarska. I didn't feel this should be sensationalized or could be re-created, so I just pasted it in as a fact and suggested we use the original ITN footage. I read what I had written and realised that it wasn't a script, but a collage. I tried to get away with it by putting in 'chapter headings' to guide the reader through it. But it was a mess.

I had a crisis of faith in the whole thing. Every film I watched seemed infinitely better. Michael, however, liked the mess. He believed he could make a film that worked not by linear narrative momentum, but by the immediacy of the action itself. He took what I did and pushed it further. He removed the helpful chapter headings. Taking his cue from the concentration camp suggestion, he peppered the film with real footage. To their credit, David Aukin and Allon Reich at Channel 4 understood and supported what we were trying to do. I was expecting script doctor notes about Henderson's character bypass and the late introduction of the main story, but they never came.

Extract 2.4: 'Going with the Floe' by Alison George

In the following article from the popular science magazine *New Scientist*, the science writer Alison George analyses the reasons for the sudden decline in numbers of the Adélie penguins in the Antarctic and what this might mean for other marine populations.

Going with **the Floe**

Adélie penguins can't survive without ice. But you can have too much of a good thing.

Antarctica is the coldest, windiest place on Earth. Every year, 20 million square kilometres of sea – an area twice the size of the US – freezes during the winter. But come October, the few scientists who have spent the winter months isolated on this frigid land are joined by an influx of summer visitors making their way towards the beaches.

The incomers waddle over the ice in short lines, or toboggan on their stomachs. Leaders stop to look around, and then head off in seemingly random directions. But these Adélie penguins know exactly where they are going – they come back to the same place every year. Soon cities of penguins will form: pockets of noise, chaos and smell in this empty continent.

With their white fronts and black heads and backs, the penguins may look like they are wearing tuxedos, but this is no party. Life in the Antarctic is harsh, and the penguins are experts in survival, moving seasonally with the ebb and flow of their icy environment. Having spent the winter on the margins between ice and sea, they need ice-free ground for their nests, and ready access to open water to feed their chicks.

The Adélie penguin's survival is intimately linked with ice, but it is a love–hate relationship. During the winter, ice is a platform to live on and the best place to find food but it can also act as a barrier, blocking access to traditional nesting grounds and feeding areas. Now, parts of the Antarctic are experiencing their own version of a heatwave, and rogue icebergs are creating havoc. Can the Adélie penguin weather the changes?

At the height of the most recent ice age, around 19,000 years ago, the ice had a stronger grip on Antarctica than it does today. A thick sheet covered the continent, extending far beyond the land and dropping off into the sea in high cliffs. Most of the Antarctic mainland was blocked off to Adélie penguins, forcing them to retreat to offshore islands. But slowly the world entered the warm interglacial phase that we're now in, and huge icebergs calved off the ice shelves, exposing rocky beaches. Adélie penguins swept southwards from their refuges to recolonise the continent. Today there are almost 5 million of them in over 150 colonies.

After the thawing ice shelves shrank back to reveal suitable beaches for Adélie penguins to nest on, their fate was controlled by another form of ice – sea ice. Outside their nesting season the birds make their home among the broken chunks of pack ice at the edge of the frozen sea. Although it appears barren, the sea ice is a vital food source for penguins. The underside is covered in a lawn of algae and the upside-down larder is full of krill – shrimp-like crustaceans that are a key food for penguins.

Antarctic sea ice always behaves erratically, and it is impossible to predict how much will form each year. But one region has experienced drastic changes that seem to be part of a longer-term trend. The Antarctic Peninsula – the horn of land extending northwards from the continent towards South America – has warmed rapidly in the past 50 years. 'Air temperatures in the west peninsula have increased dramatically, about 2.5 to 3° C since the 1950s,' says John King, from the British Antarctic Survey based in Cambridge. 'Over this timescale, it is probably the most rapid warming seen anywhere in the world.'

An increase in temperature of just a few degrees can have a huge effect on icy regions. 'The entire food chain has been affected,' says Wayne Trivelpiece, an ecologist with the US Antarctic Marine Living Resources Program in La Jolla, California. The peninsula itself has become visibly greener. Grasses and mosses are growing in places they have never been seen before. And as the air warms up the sea-ice cover is diminishing. 'The sea used to be heavily covered in ice most winters, but now the sea ice is following a cyclical pattern, with strong ice winters for two years in a row, then three to five years of warm winters with little ice,' says Trivelpiece.

It's bad news for the Adélie. For them, breeding involves long fasts, so they must build up their fat reserves during the winter if they are to successfully raise their chicks. And the sea ice is their main source of food. 'No ice means a major loss of penguins,' says Trivelpiece. Take the colonies on King George Island off the tip of the peninsula, which Trivelpiece has visited for the past 25 years. Less than half of the young penguins survive and return to breed at the colonies compared with 10 years ago. 'Something major has happened. The krill have crashed, and that's tied into the ice story,' he says. It's a similar picture at many colonies along the peninsula.

The signs are ominous. Biologists regard Adélie penguins as a vital indicator of the health of this ecosystem, a 'canary in the coal mine'. 'Adélie penguins show us what will happen to other krill-dependent species like whales and seals, which are not so easy to monitor,' says Trivelpiece.

Extract 2.5: 'Why TV for Toddlers is Good in Moderation' by Ruth Inglis

In the text which follows, taken from *eye*, a magazine for the parents and carers of young children under five, the writer analyses the effects of television viewing on toddlers.

Why TV for Toddlers is Good in Moderation

Ruth Inglis takes a look at a few toddlers' television programmes and weighs the pros and cons of allowing young children to watch such series.

Since the end of the 1990s, specific television series have been made for the very young (one- to three-year-olds). But controversy surrounds this new direction. Should toddlers be watching television, let alone series specifically made for them? Educationalists and child study experts have strong conflicting views on this matter.

The Teletubbies

Looking back, this controversy has raged ever since Anne Wood, 63, a former Warwickshire children's magazine editor, now head of Ragdoll Productions, created the *Teletubbies* in 1997.

She never made any secret of the fact that this series was specifically made for toddlers.

The series revolves around the activities of four fuzzy dolls dressed in bright, primary colours. The four (Po, Laa Laa, Dipsy and Tinky Winky) live an apparently blissful existence in a dappled meadow enveloped in sunshine and with a giggling baby laughing in a celestial aureole above their heads.

They eat Tubby toast and custard and watch the antics of human children screened on television sets centred in their tummies.

They communicate with each other in unashamed baby-talk: 'Uh oh' when their toaster springs a mechanical fault; 'eh oh' for 'hello'; 'big hug' as a babyish invitation to an embrace and 'again, again' when they want to repeat a fun activity.

Now what can be so disturbing about all this sunny activity?

Educationalists insist that toddlers should not be encouraged to talk baby-talk; to sit glued to the set while their mothers enjoy the early morning leisure break given to them by the built-in baby-sitter.

And now, perhaps most alarming of all, nutritionists are saying that toddlers are becoming obese because of this inactivity. Whether babies are getting fatter because they eat along with the 'Tubbies', or because of the resulting lack of exercise, has not yet been fully determined.

Anne Wood counters these arguments against her immensely lucrative show (aired internationally via BBC productions) by saying that her series is meticulously researched.

The Tubbies are meant to emulate toddlers' movements (Wood and her team research toddler activities in two nurseries in Warwickshire near her studio) and it is true that the Tubbies' bottom-heavy, swaying movements are the essence of toddler motion.

And she strongly rejects the idea that anything is wrong with their baby-talk. Anne Wood's defence of baby-talk is that speech is the last, not the first, piece of the language puzzle. Research shows, she insists, that movement comes first and is basic to the growth of thinking skills and ultimately to speech.

Many child development experts disagree strongly. Movement does precede speech in a toddler's development, but the salient point here is that while watching the Tubbies, the toddler is sitting transfixed, certainly not making many, if any, movements.

Their basic argument is that a toddler should not be seated motionlessly in front of the screen at all during his or her waking hours. The recent obesity figures for the under-fours merely reinforced their argument.

Anne Wood defends her Tubbies in other ways. She points out that reality also enters into the dolls' ideal world. She says she builds her programmes around 'inserts', films of real children shown in their tele-tummies. She says that the inserts are windows on the toddlers' worlds. Children in the insert films are seen engaging in real-life activities such as washing-up, riding ponies and playing in the rain.

In any case, Wood need not worry unduly, the BBC funders of her series (BBC Children, BBC Worldwide and BBC Education) seem more than satisfied with the bobbing, swaying foursome. It is a top international money-spinner.

This has not stopped some nations from turning it down. Norway led the backlash in 1998 when Ada Haug, head of pre-school programmes at NRK Norway, said she did not want it. She explained her action: 'Children are invited into an alien-looking world with some alien-looking creatures, talking in baby language. What is there for small children to aspire to grow up to?'

British child study experts are less condemning. At a conference in London in May 2002, Dr Sarah Brewer, author of *A Child's World* (2001), emphasised that young children have strong self-images from one to eighteen months (firmly saying 'I' and 'me') and can, therefore, separate themselves from what they are watching.

She said that her own toddler twins were avid viewers. 'They hug each other when the Teletubbies hug each other. I think the programme helps their social skills.'

Other programmes

Barney and Friends (Channel 5), a North American import, is one of the most popular series for toddlers and pre-schoolers in the UK and boasts a myriad of Barney clubs as well as a monthly Barney magazine.

Barney is a large purple dinosaur with a wide toothy grin who sways and dances and implores his human boy and girl friends to be polite and considerate with each other.

This amiable dinosaur has the three ingredients of children's television that appeal to very young viewers. It is colourful, kaleidoscopic and laced with rhythmic jingles. Repetition is its foundation and therefore gives young children the comfortable feeling of security that knowing what is coming next gives.

But Ellen Seiter, a communications professor at the University of California, found that numerous American day care givers, particularly the strongly Christian ones, were made uneasy by Barney's 'magical powers' (Seiter, 1999).

One parent at a Christian pre-school day care centre was especially troubled when her child announced that Barney 'was better than Jesus'. He certainly makes his 'friends' enjoy magic carpet rides all over the world when the mood takes him.

One will recall that 30-year-old veteran of pre-school television viewers, *Sesame Street* (shown on Channel 4), the lasting brain-child of the brilliant Jane Ganz Cooney. The show, with its beguiling Jim Henson puppets such as Oscar the Grouch and Big Bird, has had its severe critics.

Monica Sims, former head of BBC children's programmes, famously turned it down in the early 1970s on the grounds that it was too American.

Today *Sesame Street* has few critics, though some teachers and carers say it makes children 'passive viewers' (see again Ellen Seiter's work). However, it is frequently praised for its picture of street life in Hispanic Manhattan.

The best of the television series for children have the admirable aim of teaching tolerance of other languages, colour and creeds.

The four stars of the *Tweenies*, the BBC's series starring a rhythmic foursome, come in radiant clothes colours and skin shades and could be Irish, Swedish or Nigerian for all their big and small viewers know. Proof that television for toddlers can teach them a lot more than just the ABC.

Conclusion

Television for toddlers is a wholesome activity though child experts warn against overdoing it. Many counsel a fairly strict rationing – never more than fifteen hours a week.

And they add that watching with a parent or carer is the best antidote to passivity. Share the pleasure with the toddler and talk to him or her about what is going on on the screen.

References

Seiter, E. (1999) *Television and New Media Audiences*, Oxford University Press.
Brewer, S. (2001) *A Child's World*, Headline.

Extract 2.6: 'The Challenge to Family Life' by Jonathan Bradley and Hélène Dubinsky

The following passage is taken from a book written by two counsellors working at the Tavistock Clinic, a clinic which works with disturbed children and their families. Here the authors analyse some of the ways in which friction can develop in families as children grow into teenagers.

The dramas of teenage life are played out with great intensity in the family. From the parents' perspective, this threatens to shatter the equilibrium of family life. From the teenagers' perspective, they are waging a justified struggle for greater freedom; if parents give in too much to their imperious demands, however, teenagers are liable to feel abandoned.

Mood swings

Adolescence is characterised by intense changes of mood. These can range from sulkiness to violent rages that may prove very disturbing for the whole family. Teenagers' attempts to deal with massive internal changes can render them so volatile that they magnify the smallest quarrel. Somehow, life seems to be lived at a more intense level than previously.

To adults, it may seem that the new day brings a new person with very little in common with the teenager who was there the day before. Parents may feel that they are receiving the kind of overflow of emotion they would have known how to respond to when their children were younger: with a hug, perhaps, or a teasing joke. Suddenly it feels more awkward: responding directly to troubles, particularly in an affectionate way such as with a hug or a kiss, can embarrass teenagers and lead them to feel that they are being treated like children. Of course, sometimes a reassuring physical gesture may be what they secretly long for.

To teenagers, however, parents can seem equally unreasonable. At times they may seem willing to discuss things, treating them like an adult; while at other times, they may seem unnecessarily strict, trying to turn the clock back to when their child was younger.

Issues which may seem trivial to parents take on huge importance for teenagers (as well as vice versa!). For example, while we may think of birthdays as an occasion for celebration, teenagers may feel that they point inexorably to adulthood and in particular, towards independent living and sexual maturity. At times, the thought of growing up and taking greater responsibility is welcome to teenagers, but at others, growing up is a frightening prospect, and they may wish to remain small and dependent.

Keeping boundaries

Sometimes, parents may feel that they have failed to establish any agreement about common rules in the household, because issues on which agreement seemed to have been reached are subjected to a repeated assault. Mary explained her dilemma as follows: she wanted to acknowledge her daughter Louise's need for space, but she was also consumed with worry because at times, in wanting to stay out late, Louise seemed oblivious of danger. When questioned as to when she would come home, Louise would give a very vague answer, clearly irritated at being questioned. Phrases such as, 'It's my life', and 'I wish you would just trust me', did not calm Mary's anxiety, for although Louise fiercely defended her 'maturity', Mary could see she was at heart a vulnerable little girl. There seemed to be no way of communicating this without provoking arguments. Such confrontations happen all the time.

The pressure to relax boundaries can be enormous, as can be the temptation to impose inflexible arrangements suitable for a young child rather than a teenager. At times, it seems as though a situation could develop in which parents and teenagers are being presented with conflicting demands: on the one hand, the drive for separation and on the other hand, the drive for reassuring dependence. Both seem equally compelling. For example, if teenagers don't feel that they are being taken care of in a nurturing way, they may feel abandoned. While many adolescents will argue endlessly with whatever rules are imposed, it is very important that parents continue to set boundaries, and maintain a dialogue with their teenagers.

At times, this struggle can lead to division between parents. Jean and Charles described how they had been having trouble with Thomas, their sixteen-year-old son. Recently, he had started leaving the family, spending long hours outside. Sunday lunch had until recently been a focal point for the family. Jean described how on one occasion she put a lot of effort into making a Sunday lunch which Thomas would appreciate. She made a point of asking him what he liked and went out of her way to prepare it. Just as the lunch was about to go on the table, Thomas appeared in his coat saying that he wouldn't be in for lunch (even though he had taken part in drawing up the menu) because he was seeing his girlfriend. Out he went. To her surprise, after Thomas had gone, Charles turned on her and said that she hadn't cooked the meal Thomas liked and that was why he had gone out. Although Jean appreciated that Charles too was feeling the strain of trying to hold on to Thomas and keep him within the family, it hurt her deeply because she had put such a lot of effort into preparing the meal. Although such incidents can seem trivial, they can cause enormous rifts within families. When they talked more about it, Charles saw that he had attacked Jean because he was hurt by Thomas' rejection, and she was an easy target.

Expectations and disillusionments

During these years, teenagers are making important life decisions. This may lead parents to look back on their own lives, including its disappointments or missed opportunities.

It is possible to overburden adolescents with hopes and expectations which don't originate from them. Parents may find it particularly infuriating to be faced with their adolescent's uncertainties, preoccupation with fashion, music or friends, rather than the 'motivated' adolescent they wish to see.

Michael, for example, had grown up under the shadow of his older sister. She had excelled in her studies, gaining admission to a prestigious university. Michael had performed much less well than she had, though he had still grown up with the expectation that he would follow in the family tradition of medicine. At least three generations in the family had been doctors or specialists in medicine. Michael was able to talk to a family friend, who was puzzled by the apparent contradiction between what seemed like an intellectual liveliness and the clear evidence that Michael was doing very badly at school. In general it appeared that for Michael, still a teenager, the future had already been mapped out. It seemed to him, that within the school he attended there were many teenagers who were quite clear about their own choice of career. By contrast, his choice of career was being predetermined by family tradition. A dutiful part of him was convinced that he must follow earlier generations. At the same time, it was quite apparent that he wouldn't be able to get sufficiently high grades to do this. More than this, he had managed to get himself into a position within the class structure whereby he was regarded as a non-performer, something of a class clown who could be relied upon to enliven the proceedings by not having finished homework and by producing colourful excuses. So the stated aim, that of following in his father's footsteps, was clung to, but it had a hollow ring to it.

Recently, Michael had started to talk about his own ambitions. On the whole, they were expressed negatively, more to do with what he didn't want to do rather than with positive interest. One suggestion he made was that he should leave school early rather than proceed to 'A' levels and university. When he talked it through, however, it became obvious that he was trying to put himself into a position where he couldn't possibly be asked to pursue the family profession. How could he do this if he was a failure? It seemed hard for him to think that qualifications could lead to another profession. Michael wasn't at all confident that if he did well in exams he would be able to resist the pressure to take up medical studies.

Interestingly, when the family friend, with Michael's permission, spoke to his parents about the pressure which he felt Michael was under, it became apparent that they were unaware of what a daunting task it was for him to be expected to follow in the family footsteps. Michael's mother had experienced similar pressures in her own life but she had been able to express her rebellion in a more forthright and obvious way. She was very disillusioned by what she felt was his lack of ambition and intellectual ability. The thought that there may have been a connection between poor performance and confusion about the future was frankly a new concept to her. Once accepted, however, she was able to use her insight to reopen discussions with him about the future. There was a remarkable leap in progress once it became clear that the future was his to shape, rather than a grim mould into which he would have to be pressed and fitted.

This example is not unique. Indeed, the theme of disillusionment coupled with despair which can develop between teenagers and parents when expectations fail to be fulfilled is a common experience, but it can be negotiated when dealt with sensitively.

Writing to analyse: Activities

Before reading – oral activities

1   **Oral activity for access:**

An analysis is a way of taking something apart, looking not only at *what* it is, but also *how* and *why*. It is a kind of writing which you come across frequently in different school subjects, from history to science. Analytical writing involves looking at the way in which a process or event occurs, usually with very little personal opinion expressed.

  a In pairs or in a small group, brainstorm the process which takes a potato from growing in a farmer's field to appearing as chips for a school dinner, and then add a few notes on ways in which the process could go wrong (potatoes get a disease, they are kept in storage too long, the chips are cut too large, the oil is too old or too cold, etc.).

  b Together, note down an outline for an analysis of successful chip-making for school dinners, deciding what to include and how to present your findings.

2   **Oral activity for assessment (group interaction – explore, analyse):**

  a In a small group, choose an ordinary, everyday activity which you could do either well or badly – for instance, brushing your teeth, playing a game of football, doing your maths homework.

  b Brainstorm all the different elements which could make the activity a success or a failure.

  c Discuss together how to arrange all these elements into an analysis of how to perform your chosen activity successfully.

During reading

1 As you read the extracts in this section, look at the ways
   in which the writer or writers set out the different stages
   of the process they are discussing, and how they make
   clear how one thing follows on from the next.

   a While you are reading, note down the linking words or
     connectives that the writer uses ('then', 'because',
     'although', etc.).

   b Jot down a brief plan of the sequence of ideas in the
     text or texts you are studying, noting how the writer
     moves the analysis along.

2 When you have finished reading, note down the main
   topic of the text you have studied and then draw up an
   outline for the text, numbering each paragraph and
   writing a brief summary of what each paragraph contains
   and the way in which it moves the analysis forward.

After reading

Select a question from *either* the linked writing *or* the
coursework questions at the end of this book and follow the
instructions to help you prepare and answer the question.

Writing to review

Extract 2.7: '*Pants*: My New Book'

This is a book review from a magazine, *Junior*, for the parents and carers of young children. It is slightly different from the usual run of book reviews, in that the writer of the review has asked the illustrator of the book for his opinion of the book he has just illustrated.

PantS MY NEW BOOK

Pants by Nick Sharratt and Giles Andreae
David Fickling, hardback, £10.99, 2+

'Small pants, big pants, big frilly pig pants ...' Oh, there's nothing like a pair of pants to get the giggles going, and the latest offering from illustrator Nick Sharratt and writer Giles Andreae is dedicated to pants of every shape, colour, size and type, and then some.

So where exactly does one go to find inspiration for this saucy sort of thing? A rifle through the underwear drawer? 'Not exactly,' laughs Sharratt. 'I took my inspiration from Giles's words, but I also wanted to add visual humour. It's a delicate balance to get the right amount of cheeky humour without going over-the-top and upsetting people. The "tight pants", for example, took a few goes.

'Above all, *Pants* is supposed to be fun,' adds Sharratt. 'The best books are always those that you can read again and again, and still find something new, which is why I try to add little details in the illustrations to prompt discussion.'

And there's more to all these pants than simple humour: Andreae's wacky concepts and easy rhyme set a fast and furious pace, adding momentum as the text flows. There are also lots of educational opportunities to spot opposites, learn numbers, identify colours and animals, with a whole array of zany patterns.

'It was fun creating all the little extras, like the hidden pants in some illustrations,' says Sharratt. And, judging by the schools Sharratt has already visited with the book, the children have had just as much fun reading it. 'I couldn't believe it, but one of the schools broke into spontaneous applause at the end!' he says.

Extract 2.8: 'Science Books for Children'

The texts below are all reviews of science books for young children. As the reviews appeared in a popular science magazine, *Focus*, the writers know that their readers are interested in science and would like to share that interest with their children.

Science Books
for Children

Oxford Children's Encyclopedia of Science and Technology
Ben Dupre (ed.) (OUP £9.99)

From the zappy sparkly plasma thing on the cover to the adverts at the back, this encyclopedia is exactly what you'd expect – a summary of all kinds of science and technology, arranged in a child-friendly format. The text is clear, the photos are colourful, and the layout is clean. So why the mediocre rating? Because this is a science book designed for adults to buy for their kids, rather than a science book to amaze, enthrall and excite the kids themselves. Earnestly, self-consciously educational, but lacking in fun, humour and the essential wow factor.
Simon Adamson

Oxford First Book of Science
Nina Morgan (OUP £6.99)

A more successful attempt at involving young children in exploring the world around them, Nina Morgan gets the right balance between abstract info-dumping, play and education.

It's going to be hard for kids to resist making their own jet engine (blow up a balloon and let it go – no, it's not just a floppy rubber thing making a rude noise as it bounces off walls, ceilings and people, it's a proper experiment), playing with shadow puppets by moonlight, and working out which glass in the house is the biggest, so they can grab the most Coke at dinnertime. Not so much proper, grown-up, oh-so-serious science, as an excuse for play with some science education thrown in sneakily while the kids aren't looking. Fun, and educational too. Any remaining worries are soothed by the fact that the illustrations are properly, albeit slightly relentlessly, multicultural.
Simon Adamson

Science Basics
Graham Peacock and Jill Jesson (Letts £3.99)

This hands-on series, having activities written with the National Curriculum in mind, and aimed at five- to eleven-year-olds, is an inventive mix of practical experiments, quizzes and challenges. Each book, aimed at a particular age group, is packed with fun and fascinating experiments which appeal to young and eager minds. Each page begins with a 'Look and Learn' section which details an interesting scientific principle or fact and explains, in very simple terms, why and how it works. This could be anything from why the Earth orbits the Sun, or how vibrations cause sounds, to creating an electrical circuit, or investigating the properties of heat. This is followed by a 'Practice' section for testing your new-found knowledge and a 'Challenge' section of home-based experiments. There are lots of opportunities for parental involvement, too.
David Frisby

Our World – Questions and Answers Encyclopedia
John Farndon, Colin Hynson, Ian James and Angela Royston
(Marks & Spencer £5)

You know how it is. You are out and about with the kids when suddenly, out of nowhere, one of them asks a question that leaves you stumped. It's not that you can't answer the question (of course you can), it's just that you don't know the best way to do it so that they can grasp what you mean. The answer, fortunately, lies in this book – or, rather, within the hundreds of child-friendly answers it contains to some mind-boggling questions. If your kids have ever asked you what an atom is or how we can see through our eyes, you'll find the answers here. It's the sort of book that can keep young minds engrossed for hours and keep them coming back for more.
Gail Lowther

Extract 2.9: 'New Theroux'

This review, which appeared in the *Geographical* magazine, is written for people who are interested in faraway places, and probably already know the work of the popular travel writer Paul Theroux – so the reviewer doesn't need to explain who Theroux is, just what he has written about in his new book.

New **Theroux**

Dark Star Safari: Overland from Cairo to Cape Town
Paul Theroux (Hamish Hamilton, hb, pp. 512, £17.99)

Many people who visit Africa go on safari in the hope of seeing the 'Big Five' in the vast expanses of the Serengeti or Masai Mara. But Paul Theroux isn't most people. As if to counter the negative image of the continent that is often presented to us in the media – the predictable stories of famine, poverty, violence, disease and corruption – Theroux sets out on an overland journey from Cairo to Cape Town.

Having worked as a teacher in Malawi and Uganda nearly 40 years ago, he's compelled to return to discover the truth for himself. Against the better judgement of locals and government embassies, Theroux treks on, braving over-stuffed buses and intimidating border guards.

In the metaphorical company of the great explorers and writers of the past, Theroux describes the experiences, opinions, mind-sets and moods of his journey. Sadly, he encounters plenty of evidence of a continent much diminished since his first visit. He concludes that it is 'hungrier, poorer, less educated, more pessimistic, more corrupt', and that 'you can't tell the politicians from the witch-doctors'. Nevertheless, Theroux's journey is fascinating and provides a real insight into an Africa few of us will experience.

Winnie Liesenfeld

Extract 2.10: 'Inside Advertising' by Peter Souter

The text below is a review which appeared in *Campaign* magazine, the 'inhouse' magazine for the British advertising industry, in which each week an advertising executive is invited to give their opinion of current advertising campaigns. Here Peter Souter offers his views on a range of campaigns from BT broadband to the Royal National Institute for the Blind. He starts off by establishing himself as an 'insider' by talking about various figures, past and present, in the advertising industry.

Inside ADVERTISING

Al Young fascinates me. Not the Al Young who used to work with Trevor Robinson and won all the prizes in the early nineties. He got there first and is therefore relatively normal. The Al Young who concerns me is the one making such a splendid job of running St Luke's Advertising Agency.

Why doesn't he change his name?

Even going to Alan Young would make a difference. Or perhaps Will Young, then at least he'd get mixed up with someone in a different line of work. What about Crosby Stills Nash and Young?

Nobody is really using that any more and he'd sound like an ad agency all on his own.

Anyway, for reasons best known to himself, Al Young pays no heed to the cock-up on his business cards and gets on with creating nice BT commercials.

Last year's 'arena' spot pulled off the difficult trick of being massive and intimate at the same time. Didn't you love the Table Mountain clouds that rolled over the top of the stadium? This year's outing is a burst broadband pipe that lets a stream of digital goodies shoot out into the sky. A pig, a basketball, a rhino, the space shuttle, some characters my son Teddy assures me are from Tekken. The only people who come out of the ground looking shamefaced are the computer wizards whose three-headed monster looks embarrassingly bad. Jarvis 'in your own time' Cocker is a much better use of our phone bills. No need to tell you any more because BT is spending a million pounds a day on running it so you'd have to be blind not to have seen it.

If you are blind and a friendly if rather cruel person is currently reading out *Campaign* to you, get them to stop and read out the copy on the RNIB's new ads instead. I'm sure you'll be moved, as I was, to discover that someone has thought of a novel way of getting that fine organisation some much-needed attention.

You might wish you couldn't see if you'd been forced to watch the Nestlé Double Cream ad as many times as I have. And I've only watched it once.

Clarks has got itself a neat little commercial, though. Lots of ordinary people doing that extraordinarily stupid walk that models do in fashion shows. 'Remember life's one long catwalk' thrills the endline. Sweet, although a bit light on actual shoes. As this is another one from Al's agency, maybe he can get Clark's to rebrand itself Nike?

Remember when Tom Carty and Walter Campbell used to write the Kiss 100 ads? They were Livesexy without ever having to say they were. Just a thought. I like the daring of the team on this ad but I think they have lost a little of the warmth and surprise in the original 'Boss turns into pussy cat' execution.

Finally we have the Ben and Jerry's campaign, my favourite ads of the week. If I had written 'We reserve the right to turn our leftovers into whole new flavours', I'd give myself a small but gratifying pay rise and take the rest of the day off.

Extract 2.11: 'Romancing the Holocaust' by Robert S. Leventhal

The following text is taken from a website put up by the University of Virginia in the United States. In it Robert S. Leventhal gives his view of Steven Spielberg's film *Schindler's List*. He is profoundly uneasy about the Hollywood portrayal of the complex tragedy which was the Holocaust, in which six million Jews were systematically massacred by the Nazi regime during the Second World War.

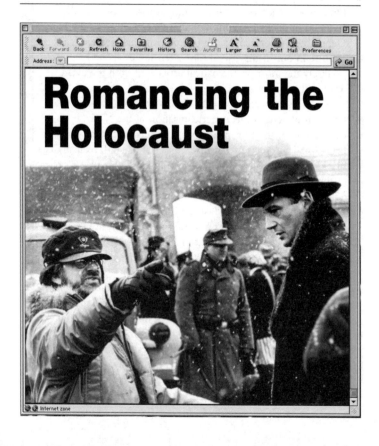

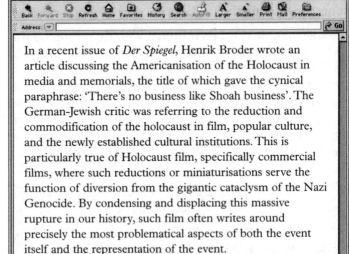

In a recent issue of *Der Spiegel*, Henrik Broder wrote an
article discussing the Americanisation of the Holocaust in
media and memorials, the title of which gave the cynical
paraphrase: 'There's no business like Shoah business'. The
German-Jewish critic was referring to the reduction and
commodification of the holocaust in film, popular culture,
and the newly established cultural institutions. This is
particularly true of Holocaust film, specifically commercial
films, where such reductions or miniaturisations serve the
function of diversion from the gigantic cataclysm of the Nazi
Genocide. By condensing and displacing this massive
rupture in our history, such film often writes around
precisely the most problematical aspects of both the event
itself and the representation of the event.

Steven Spielberg's epic film *Schindler's List* (1994) is the
latest instalment in this Americanisation of the Nazi
destruction of the European Jews, and it is particularly
problematical precisely because, for all of its stark realism, its
black and white contrast, and its unflinching look in the eye
of the process of mass murder, it remains, in the final
analysis, a Hollywood romance, mourning on the screen in a
sentimental and nostalgic fashion. The condensation and
displacement of *Schindler's List* are most evident in Oskar
Schindler's psychic investment in and the over-
determination of the only colour image in the entire film,
that of the little girl in the red coat.

It is one image in particular that condenses all of the Nazi
sadism into one small pictorial area, a displacement of the
mass murder of millions of people to a tiny remnant, a red
coat of a small girl, one of the few colour images in the
entire film that bounces through the streets of Krakow until
we finally see her mangled body and the red coat being

carried on a small wagon as Amon Göth and his crew orchestrate the burning of the last traces of the remains of the murdered prisoners. Oskar Schindler follows this image in a visual romance until he finally sees her body, at which point his conscience is miraculously brought to life, a moral reawakening that slowly but surely changes his capitalist fantasies into a singular dedication to save as many Jews as possible.

Schindler's List is an important cinematic event, for it does mark the first explicit, self-conscious portrayal of the Holocaust in a major Hollywood film. The colour images of the film contrast with the harsh black and white footage that begins with the escalation of the war against the Jews. The key colour image of the little girl marks the eclipse of humanity, and Schindler, the voyeur who witnesses the liquidation of the Ghetto from a hill, stands as a powerful reminder of the bystanders who looked on as the Nazi Genocide of the Jews proceeded. Finally, it is possible to grasp the implications of the making of the film itself when we remember that Spielberg had wanted to film at Auschwitz, but was convinced by the World Jewish Organisation among others of the inappropriateness of such action; one cannot make films where Jewish people are buried. While we must acknowledge the educational function *Schindler's List* serves for a society that is only remotely aware of the Nazi Genocide in its bureaucratic perniciousness and technological bestiality, we have an obligation to articulate where the film falls into accepted conventions of narrative and representation, where it colludes with the logic of reduction, condensation, compression, concentration and 'levelling' that are the trademarks of Fascism itself.

Writing to review: Activities

Before reading – oral activities

1   Oral activity for access:

   a   In pairs or in a small group, select a TV programme, computer game or album track that you are all familiar with.

   b   Discuss what is good about your selected media product, and what you didn't like about it – remember to always give specific reasons for your views.

2   Oral activity for assessment (individual extended contribution – explain, describe, narrate):

a   On your own, select two or three reviews of a book, band or TV programme that you are familiar with.

b   Go through the reviews, noting down the different views and the ways in which the writers back up their views with references.

c   Work out what, in your view, makes a successful review – facts about the subject being reviewed, information, opinions, a balance of views, lively writing, etc.

d   Explain your findings to the class or to a large group, backing up your views with evidence from your research.

During reading

1   As you read the extracts in this section, look at the ways in which the writer or writers give the reader the following elements.

- information about the book, advertisement or film they are reviewing
- their own personal opinions
- close references and quotations to back up their views.

2 **a** When you have finished reading, spend a little time in pairs or in a group looking at how the writer or writers of the extracts you have studied have shaped what they have said to their target readership. You might like to consider:

- tone
- choice of language
- sentence and paragraph structure.

b Make a few notes to summarise your findings.

After reading

Select a question from *either* the linked writing *or* the coursework questions at the end of this book and follow the instructions to help you prepare and answer the question.

Writing to comment

Extract 2.12: *Sixth Form Choices* by John Handley

The following extract comes from a textbook on how to make career choices about sixth-form options and beyond. Here the writer John Handley, former Senior Careers Adviser at the University of Liverpool, comments on the different experiences of two young people.

One decision can lead to another almost without us realising what is happening. Becoming aware of the choices we are inevitably called upon to make can help to give us a sense of purpose. One of the early decisions we have to make is what kind of post-16 study we want to do.

Making choices inevitably leads on to other choices. No matter how difficult it may prove to be, having a choice gives one a positive feeling – a sense of freedom. In contrast, having no choice at all is akin to a feeling of despair, almost of imprisonment. To make a sound choice for you as an individual you need two things: good information and a good understanding of your own motivation. Two true stories, which unfolded within 24 hours of each other, will illustrate what I mean.

Jennifer's story

Late one afternoon, Jennifer came to see me. She had been very successful at school gaining four A levels with grades ranging from A to C, she had entered the university of her choice and was well into her first year reading a joint honours course in English and French. The trouble was she was not enjoying it. Joint honours courses are known to be demanding, so I queried the workload – was it too much? No, she assured me that was no problem, it was the English itself she was finding difficult.

Upon further questioning it became apparent that she felt the subject was too vague and imprecise. Clearly there is nothing wrong with choosing an academic subject like English if you are interested and enjoy it. Indeed, the subject has plenty of followers. In 1991 alone nearly 2,700 people graduated in this subject at university, even excluding those like Jennifer who were doing it in combination with another subject.

However, it is quite another matter if you discover, as Jennifer had done, that you really had no affinity with seventeenth-century English literature. In view of this, one wondered why she had chosen such a course. It emerged that she had liked the subject, and she had done well at both GCSE and A level, gaining a grade A in the latter. In the French half of her degree course, which she preferred and where consequently she was getting better marks, she had also done well, gaining a grade B at A level.

The two arts A levels seemed therefore to be her two best subjects, but to complicate matters she had also gained grade Cs in mathematics and physics. Clearly there was another aspect to Jennifer's ability and personality which had been sidelined. Now, as her first year drew to a close she was considering changing her course.

Geoff's story

My second story emerged the next morning when Geoff's father came to see me. He explained that Geoff had gained an upper second in economics, but had not managed to get a job offer. Nearly a year later he was working temporarily as a hospital porter. Now, along had come the offer of a one-year postgraduate master's degree that would give exemption from the examinations of the Royal Institute of Chartered Surveyors. Geoff's father understandably wanted to know if it would prove a good investment. With no grants available for this type of course at postgraduate level, it was clearly going to cost Geoff's family a lot of money – a sum approaching five figures was mentioned. Nor could successful completion of such a course guarantee a job. In view of this it was important to look at the young man's motivation and interest.

Obviously the next stage was to see Geoff. He was in good company: a rising proportion of graduates are going along the postgraduate route as they face an increasingly competitive job market – the latest estimates put the proportion of graduates going on to further full-time training at about one in four. The crucial question was this, did Geoff really want to be a chartered surveyor? Upon questioning him I found he knew surprisingly little about the career, and had not been talking to any practitioners. What jobs had he been applying for while still a student? Apparently he had been trying for marketing, personnel and financial jobs. He was frankly delighted and surprised to be offered a place on the master's course after so much disappointment. One sensed a feeling of relief in Geoff's family, and yet one was left wondering if it was indeed a case of any port in a storm.

Lessons to be drawn

In both of these stories there is a common thread. There was uncertainty in the minds of both Jennifer and Geoff. Jennifer's all-round ability had contributed to her uncertainty, and she and her school had been overly influenced by her academic performance at the expense of her interests and practical nature. At my request she undertook an interest inventory which seeks to measure one's reactions to various activities, and thereby produce a hierarchy of interests. The result showed that she had a marked preference for working in structural situations where the outcome was often clearly apparent. It was scarcely a recipe for seventeenth-century English literature and she has now switched to material science – one of the engineering disciplines.

Geoff too had wavered over where his interests lay, and in applying for such a wide range of jobs he had revealed his own uncertainty. It's quite possible that employers to whom he had applied had either picked this up on his application form, or had sensed it at interview. Geoff was not only intelligent, he was an active person, an athlete who enjoyed sport and was blessed with an outgoing personality. He obviously liked meeting people. With hindsight it looks as though surveying could be the ideal choice assuming he can develop the necessary commercial acumen. The economics degree provides a good theoretical base for what he is about to embark upon. However, one wonders whether an earlier awareness of his own inclinations and preferences would have suggested an alternative to economics? This is why every sixth-former and student should be encouraged to explore and experience as many activities as possible outside the curriculum, and not just regard themselves as chemists, economists, or whatever.

It pays to always take account of the true nature of your interests alongside your subject preferences before selecting your sixth-form subjects.

Extract 2.13: 'Grey Goo' by Steve Connor

The text below is taken from the editorial pages of the broadsheet newspaper, *The Independent*. In this article, Steve Connor comments on contemporary attitudes to 'nanotechnology', particularly amongst those he describes as the 'posh end of the ecology movement'.

Grey Goo

Who's afraid of a miniaturised Raquel Welch?

There was a time when the word 'nanotechnology' would have newspaper picture editors reaching for photographs of Raquel Welch. The one where Welch adorns the crew of the miniaturised submarine in the 1960s film *Fantastic Voyage*. For those too young to remember, the sub is sent on a mission to explore the arteries and veins of an important diplomat dying from a blood clot.

Making Raquel Welch small enough to fit inside something the size of a pinhead is just about as realistic as the possibility of 'grey goo' gobbling up the world. Grey goo is the latest phrase to describe the obliteration of life on Earth resulting from the spread of swarms of self-replicating robots, or 'nanobots', the size of bacteria – a silicon version of the Sars virus.

Some people are really worried about the grey goo
scenario. Prince Charles and Zac Goldsmith – the posh end of
the ecology movement – are concerned enough to question
the direction of nanotechnology and say ethical concerns are
not being addressed as fast as the research is proceeding.
Grey goo angst is the next step for both those who worry
about the release of GM microbes and those who criticise
scientists for playing God with living, or indeed, non-living
things.

Prince Charles, who has asked the Royal Society for advice
about individuals who could speak on developments in
nanotechnology, has evidently been reading a report called
The Big Down, published by the Etc Group, a Canadian
organisation investigating the social and cultural implications
of new technology. The authors of The Big Down report refer
to nanotechnology as 'Atomtech' and are in little doubt that it
poses a credible threat to civilisation as we know it.

'Atomtech could mean the creation and combination of
new elements and the amplification of weapons of mass
destruction.'

The report goes on to ask: what if submicroscopic
'nanobots' start replicating and don't stop? 'The self-
replicating and assembly processes could go haywire until the
world is annihilated by nanobots or their products. Grey goo
refers to the obliteration of life that could result from the
accidental and uncontrollable spread of self-replicating
assemblers,' it says.

Now at this point it would be good to distinguish fact from
fiction. First, nanotechnology is not some magical science that
has appeared from nowhere. It is merely an extension of the
'micro' technology that has fashioned and shaped the late
twentieth century. A nanometre is a billionth of a metre
(about 1/80,000 of the diameter of a human hair) and
nanotechnology is a catch-all description of anything
constructed or manipulated at this submicroscopic level.

It was Richard Feynman, the great American physicist and
sometime bongo player, who first raised the possibility of

working at this level, when he gave his 1959 lecture to the American Physical Society entitled There is plenty of room at the bottom. Eric Drexler expanded on this in his book Engines of Creation; in 1981 he coined the term 'nanotechnology'.

There are two different approaches to nanotechnology. One is 'bottom up', which envisages building things atom upon atom, and the other is 'top down', which is based on the idea of making nanoscale structures by etching out or machining existing larger structures, in much the same way as computer chips are now made.

Few observers doubt the immense rewards that could come about by continued miniaturisation – a trend that has affected everything from computers to drug development. Scientists have already created single-molecule transistors, and an enzyme-powered, bio-molecular motor with nickel propellers and a tiny carrier able to cross the vital barrier between the blood and the brain.

But no one has come near to miniaturising anything inanimate to replicate along the lines of the grey goo scenario. 'It's all just nonsense,' says Sir Harry Kroto, who won a Nobel prize for his work on molecular balls of carbon atoms – structures that can be used to make nanoscale tubes.

'Nanotechnology is basically chemistry of the twenty-first century. People who suggest it will lead to self-replicating robots have no idea what is needed for self-replication. It's a total lunacy,' says the exasperated laureate. Even Richard Smalley, a Nobel laureate at Rice University in Houston, Texas, who has said that nanotechnology will become more important than the combined influence of microelectronics, medical imaging and man-made polymers, believes that self-replicating nanobots are 'simply not possible in our world'.

Yet the image of grey goo taking over the world – although not as photogenic as that of Raquel Welch squeezing into a mini-sub – is set to become another fixed image in the public mind. But I wonder which grey goo we're talking about? That resulting from a nanobot meltdown or the stuff that sits between the ears of some of the higher-bred eco-warriors?

Extract 2.14: *Losing It* by Malcolm Campbell

This text provides a fairly detailed commentary on a Channel 4 schools drama called *Losing It*. In this text, which appeared on the Channel 4 website, the writers present the plot of the drama and some of the thinking behind it.

Losing It is a 4Learning drama about young people and mental health.

Young people with mental health problems are likely to feel very isolated and distressed. It is important for them to know that help is available and that they are not alone. And the sooner problems are tackled, the easier they are to deal with and the less they will disrupt everyday life.

Losing It: an outline

People of all ages can find the subject of mental health difficult, frightening and alienating. The starting point of the programme is that mental health problems of different degrees of severity can affect anyone at any time in their lives.

There was particular concern to locate the drama in the kind of everyday experiences that anyone might have. The writer Malcolm Campbell created three young characters – Jude, Tom and Muna – whose lives connect powerfully for one week. From the outset, they seem no more or less complex or troubled than many other young people their age. But behind the front that we all construct to the rest of the world, one of the three, Jude, is experiencing difficulties ...

A reckless edge

Bright, good-looking, athletic and eighteen years old, Jude has a reckless edge that makes him both attractive and dangerous. We quickly learn that, behind the image he presents to the world, he is experiencing difficulties with academic work. Exams, which he sees as his passport out, are imminent and he's been struggling.

He enlists the help of Tom, a student in his psychology class, to help him study. Tom and Jude know each other but they are not really friends. It's unlikely Tom has much social life at all because he has been caring for his mother who is recovering from depression. Academically a high achiever, independent, self-reliant but a bit of a loner, he is intrigued and slightly flattered by Jude's request for help. Jude is also able to capitalise on Tom's infatuation with Muna, a young woman currently working as a local radio presenter: if Tom will help him prepare for the psychology exam, Jude will help Tom win Muna.

Trying to escape

Muna is sharp, quick-witted, outspoken – in Jude's words, a 'motormouth'. She seems an unlikely partner for Tom, but in the end, he gets to her without Jude's help. Tom lacks the confidence to ask Muna out in person, but he is more than capable of finding the right words to interest her via an internet chatroom. They fix a date.

The night of Tom's date with Muna is the night before the psychology exam. Tom is too nervous and excited about the evening ahead to pick up on Jude's distracted state of mind. When Jude is left alone to revise, we start to see that he is lost, troubled, even in pain. He can't concentrate, can't focus. He has to escape the room. While Tom waits for Muna, Jude goes running – trying to escape from the problems and pressures building up inside. When he returns, he seems to be on the point of turning to his parents, but, at the last moment, he can't find the words.

Still waiting, Tom calls Muna's show and manages to break through her tough-talking on-air persona. His

question, 'Are you really so cold or is it just a front?' is
disconcerting, and the call shakes Muna's confidence.

No comfort

Jude, meanwhile, has escaped the house a second time
and is drinking with his mates. But it is clear he is
unhappy, alienated, out of it. There's no comfort here, no
conversation ... Jude is very much alone.

Muna goes looking for her 'secret' date at the agreed
meeting-place and finds Tom. Intrigued by both his
phone call and his persistence, she agrees to have a drink
with him.

Hiding in the toilets at the pub, Jude hears his mates
talking about him.

Muna tries to explain why she stood Tom up and is
clearly surprised by his responses. He refuses to fit the
stereotype she has constructed for him, and she finds
herself able to drop her guard and let a little vulnerability
show through.

Walking the streets and chatting, they come across
Jude, who has taken a beating from some unknown lads.
There is a moment, when Muna touches his face, when
Jude could possibly open up to them both, but it passes
and he refuses any help, reassures them that he's fine,
and disappears before they can stop him. But the story he
has told them is at odds with what really happened. Jude
was no innocent victim of a street fight – he had actively
provoked the beating.

The hardest bit

Jude and Tom sit their exam the next morning.
Afterwards, at home, Jude hears Tom calling for him,
asking Jude if he wants to talk, saying the teacher has
been looking for him. His mother's anxious voice can be
heard on the answerphone. He goes looking for Muna,

who is having the worst possible day at the office. Jude is there waiting for her when she leaves.

Tom, too, tries to find Muna with a Woody Allen video to share, but when he discovers her at her flat with Jude, he walks out. Muna goes after him to try and explain. She had been sacked from her job and run into Jude, and they had tried to take comfort in each other. Reaching a kind of understanding, Tom and Muna return to the flat to find that Jude has taken an overdose.

In hospital, Jude talks for the first time about how he's been feeling – hurting, desperate, alone, frightened he is going mad.

Some time later, we see Jude once more. He's different. Although he's sure it's not all over, he's done the hardest bit – asked for help. And these days he can't stop talking as he tries to make sense of the past and looks forward to some kind of future.

Some key issues in *Losing It*
Definitions of mental health and mental illness
Losing It takes as its starting point the idea of viewing mental health as a continuum, ranging from stress and anxiety, through simple and clinical depression, eating and obsessive-compulsive disorders to self-harm/suicide, schizophrenia and trauma. Mental health problems can affect anyone, but it's important to recognise that some people are more vulnerable than others.

Identifying the signs of a mental health problem
The central character Jude is concealing his anxiety, distress, loneliness and feelings of worthlessness. Because he is widely regarded as capable and confident, an achiever – someone who gets on with his life – family and friends don't see anything worrying in his behaviour. This is partly because they don't expect it and partly

because Jude tries to conceal what is happening to him. The situation is complicated because Jude doesn't actually know what is happening to him.

What are some of the symptoms of a mental health problem?

Although Jude's condition is never labelled, he is depressed. In the drama, he experiences some of the more common symptoms of depression: sleeplessness, restlessness, feelings of worthlessness, sudden mood changes, difficulty in concentrating. He is also spending quite a bit of time alone in his room. On the other hand, he drives himself hard – running, forcing himself to socialise and taking risks that lead to a kind of self-harm: getting himself beaten up.

Gender and mental health

Jude doesn't talk to anyone about his feelings. Being unable to cope is both terrifying and shameful to him. Like many young men, he doesn't have the language or confidence to articulate his feelings. This is not to say that young women don't conceal things, too, but Jude's friendships (until Tom) appear to function on the public and social rather than the private and intimate level. There is no obvious support structure among the young men he goes around with.

Tom provides a different perspective – he is more emotionally expressive. However, he is socially very shy and, at the point we meet him, preoccupied with a girl. Perhaps he could help Jude but, through a mix of circumstances, both let opportunities for confidences go by.

The causes of the mental health problem

There is no sense in the drama of exactly what 'caused'

Jude's depression. The focus is deliberately on the experience of it rather than the factors that might have contributed to it. But in Jude's life there are signs of intense loneliness and a lack of intimacy, of feelings of low self-worth, of exam pressures and of fear of the future.

Losing It avoids signalling strong personal and social 'causes' such as a dysfunctional family, bereavement or social disadvantage, so that there is no neat equation of cause and effect.

Getting help

The drama goes no further than showing Jude starting on a process – hopefully towards recovery. The key is the ability to talk about the problem, and *Losing It* makes it clear that this is difficult for a variety of reasons. But in the end, Jude takes two of the most important steps: acknowledging the problem and asking for help.

Extract 2.15: 'Victoria Climbié' by Fiona Bruce

The extract below is from an article written by Fiona Bruce, newsreader and Crimewatch presenter, for *Good Housekeeping* magazine. In the article, she comments on her thoughts and feelings about the short life and tragic death of Victoria Climbié, a little girl from the Ivory Coast tortured to death in London by her great-aunt. Fiona Bruce wrote the article after she visited Victoria's parents on the Ivory Coast.

Victoria **Climbié**

I felt ashamed when they asked me how a little girl could be tortured to death in Britain without anyone noticing.

In this exclusive article written after she visited Victoria Climbié's Ivory Coast home, BBC newsreader Fiona Bruce questions whether a life in prosperous, educated Britain is really better than the love and sense of family Fiona found in poverty-ridden Africa.

The first thing you notice as you stand at the simple graveside of eight-year-old Victoria Climbié is the sound of the waves rolling on the Ivory Coast shore just a hundred yards away. It's a beautiful and peaceful place. Many of the graves are just mounds of earth; for Victoria, the Climbié family bought the finest grave they could afford. A coffin-shaped oblong, covered in what look like green bathroom tiles. There's no name on it, but they intend to laminate a photo of Victoria and stick it to one of the tiles. This is her final resting place.

The flat in north London where she spent the last few months of her life – alone in a freezing bath, without food, lying in her own excrement – couldn't be a greater contrast. The smears of her blood were found on the walls of every room, and she had 128 separate injuries, the evidence of countless beatings. Victoria's death at the hands of her great-aunt Marie-Thérèse Kouao and her boyfriend on 25 February 2000 will go down as one of the worst cases of child abuse Britain has ever seen. One which exposed the shameful failings not just of social services, but also the police, hospital consultants, religious leaders, even the NSPCC. The Laming inquiry, which has spent months poring over every detail of how Victoria's abuse was so shockingly ignored, is due to present its findings to ministers within the next few weeks.

In June, the BBC asked me to go to Ivory Coast, a poor but peaceful state in West Africa, to talk to Victoria's parents, Francis and Berthe. The resulting interview will be broadcast on BBC's 4x4 as soon as the Laming inquiry reports. I wanted to understand why they'd sent their daughter thousands of miles away to a relative, but I dreaded it. As a mother, I could hardly bear to read the inquiry cuttings – how on earth could I discuss Victoria's death with her parents?

Their house is in a suburb of Abidjan, the Ivory Coast capital, which is hot, noisy and chaotic. They live along a dirt track, in a block of three-room houses. The track is everyone's front garden. When I arrived, there were kids playing, lads sitting around a table, intent on their card game, music blaring from a ghetto blaster. A young woman was having her hair braided, another was selling a few white bread rolls in a tray.

Francis and Berthe came out to greet me, surrounded by their six remaining children. We chatted just to break the ice and gradually the music got louder, the children began to dance and within half an hour there was a party going on. And I thought, this is what Victoria left behind for the horror of that flat in London. Poverty, for sure – many of the children were in little better than rags. But they were all healthy, and there was an unmistakeable atmosphere of warmth and love. Everything was shared, everyone seemed to be looking out for everyone else. There was a true sense of community.

I asked Francis and Berthe why they'd sent Victoria away. The answer was simple: 'La petite,' as they call her, was exceptionally bright and the local school has almost no teaching materials. Only in Europe, they believed, could she have a decent education and a better future. It was a terrible wrench to let her go but they trusted Francis' aunt, Marie-Thérèse, implicitly. It's a well-trodden path, too – those who have 'rich' relatives in Europe often send their children to live with them to give them the best chance in life. It has horrible echoes of little Damilola Taylor whose family came to Britain seeking a brighter future but whose life also ended in tragedy.

When I used to read the story of Victoria daily on the Six O'Clock News, I asked myself how her parents could bear to listen to the harrowing details at the inquiry. Berthe tells me she cried every day. But her guilt at not being there to help her daughter before she died was such that she had to be there afterwards to try to understand why. When Berthe and Francis asked me how it was possible that a little girl could be tortured to death in a country as prosperous and educated as Britain, without notice or help, I felt ashamed. Berthe said she took comfort in her belief that the inquiry's conclusions will mean it could never happen again. I wish I shared her faith.

What is it about our society, I wondered, that children can be murdered so callously? We've set up an apparatus of officialdom – social workers, teachers, health visitors – so that no child should fall through the net of our own neglect, but it fails. Could such abuse happen in Africa where the responsibility falls almost entirely on the parents? There's one thing I'm sure of: even if Victoria's aunt had looked after her, even if she had been better off academically and financially in London, I don't believe Victoria would ever have found the warmth and sense of community she had at home.

I often sat with the Climbiés in their small front room dominated by a four-foot high portrait of Victoria. Francis told me that seeing her face every day makes her spirit seem closer. Berthe suffers from depression now and still cries often. Francis' business went bust when Victoria died and he's been unable to find a job. Yet they carry on – their family is strong and they have a deep faith in God, which the events in London have somehow made stronger.

Berthe believes in forgiveness. I asked her whether she'd been able to forgive Marie-Thérèse. She paused. Francis intervened quickly to say that he did, that what had happened was God's will. Berthe was still quiet. I wondered how it could be God's will to send a bright, innocent little girl into the hands of such evil. Eventually, Berthe's response was fierce. She knew God would forgive Marie-Thérèse, as he forgives all sinners, but Marie-Thérèse was an animal, not fit to live among humans, and what comforted her was the knowledge that such an animal was in prison for life. The Climbiés are now trying to raise money for a new school so that children like Victoria don't have to go away for an education. Certainly, they'll never send away another of their own.

One story that Berthe told will remain with me. Victoria had been in hospital a few months before she died. The doctor had mistaken her terrible injury scars for scabies. A nurse said that when she'd tried to give Victoria a bath, she couldn't find any way of lifting her without touching her wounds. As Victoria could only speak French, a French-speaking nurse was found. She asked Victoria if there was anything she wanted. It must have seemed to Victoria that at last, here was a way out of the hell she was enduring. She told the nurse she wanted to go home. To Victoria's joy, the nurse replied that she could. Victoria got out of bed, gathered her pitiful belongings and stood to attention by her hospital bed, waiting for her parents to walk through the door and take her home. But it was Marie-Thérèse who walked in. The nurse had misunderstood and Victoria's face just crumpled. That was one of the many missed chances to save her life.

Thinking of my welcome from Berthe and Francis I marvelled that they'd managed to find some peace despite their suffering. All they wanted was to give their daughter a way out of poverty. But that dream was what led to her death. I'll never forget Victoria's story, and I'll tell it to as many people as I can as my own small way of keeping her memory alive.

Extract 2.16: *The Political Animal* by Jeremy Paxman

The following extract is taken from a book by journalist and Newsnight presenter, Jeremy Paxman, in which he enquires into the particular qualities which drive people to take up and continue in politics in England. Here he comments on the qualities needed to become a politician in the first place.

Where did they all come from, this extraordinary breed? Once upon a time, they must have been normal. Can they really have sprung from their mothers' wombs full of doctrinaire certainties? Confronted by their mother with a plate of mashed banana at the age of two, did they exclaim, 'I congratulate the honourable lady on her choice of acceptable food for an infant. She will doubtless be aware of the vital importance of the banana trade to many member states of the Commonwealth. And will she join with me in protesting at the American government's attempt to force the World Trade Organization to capitulate to the interests of the American banana growers who provide such enormous donations to the Republican presidential campaign?' From some political memoirs, you might think they did.

In a strict sense, politicians are not like the rest of us. Whether they have been driven into political careers by a simple desire to represent their community in parliament or, like Margaret Thatcher, from a conviction that they alone could save their country, wielding power is essential. Mercifully, the proportion of people in any society who wish to tell everyone else what to do is limited. If it were not so, the country would be ungovernable. The arrangement works only because the people willing, however grudgingly, to do as they're told vastly outnumber the people who wish to order them about. Once upon a time, our leaders must have seemed normal. As babies, they bawled and mewed, they messed their nappies, and later they learned to speak and write. It was only later that they decided to make history.

Most of them seem to see themselves as adventurers. Theirs is a Dick Whittington journey which will take them from obscurity to high office, where they will make brave and wise decisions for the benefit of the nation, until they retire, garlanded with honour, knighthood or peerage, to bask in the affectionate respect of the people whose lives they have enhanced. Small wonder that parliament is filled with people preoccupied with their own image and who see the business of politics as being about who's up, who's down, who's in, who's out. In such an environment, as the Conservative MP Christopher Hollis remarked half a century ago, 'What brings a man to the top is not superior ability but – much more often – an intense desire for success, that extra little ounce of ambition that is not quite sane.'

But what is the purpose of this slightly deranged ambition? To what end, the life-plan which runs from GCSE and A Level, university, through a good marriage, good job, fine children, to MP, Minister and Prime Minister? When John Major came to reflect on what had brought him from Brixton to Westminster, he remembered the name of a now long-forgotten novel based on Ramsay MacDonald, another Prime Minister who rose from obscurity and ended his career condemned by much of his party as a traitor. '*Fame is the Spur*,' wrote Howard Spring. He was right. Political life is stimulated by ambition, and providing ambition is not obsessive, I see nothing wrong in that. Even in these cynical days it is something to be a member of Parliament, with those precious initials after your name. Success in all fields is driven by ambition. This usually involves being seen to be better than others. In politics, where the acclamation and failure are the most public of all, the prize on offer is *significance*. The desire is for recognition, the acknowledgement by other humans of the worth of the individual. Persuading thousands – or, in the case of party leaders, millions – of fellow human beings to give you their votes is one of the greatest forms of recognition available. As a young MP explained, 'Standing on the platform as the Returning Officer announces the results, knowing that the people have chosen you, is the greatest, warmest feeling. It makes you feel life is worth living. I have never, ever, felt more alive than when I was first elected as an MP.'

Writing to comment: Activities

Before reading – oral activities

1 Oral activity for access:

Most people have views on most things, from Manchester United to tomato soup. Some views are strongly held ('I can't stand mashed parsnips!'), while some are barely a preference ('I don't mind walking to the shops'). When you are commenting on something, you are simply giving your view, without necessarily wanting to persuade anybody else to agree with you.

a In a pair or a small group, brainstorm a list of things about which you hold opinions, and put them in a rank order from opinions you hold very strongly ('Harry Potter is the best thing since sliced bread') to opinions you barely hold at all ('Tomato salad is OK').

b Choose one topic each, and tell each other your opinion, and your reason for it ('I don't like sardines: they remind me of when I was ill as a kid and I had to take cod-liver oil').

2 Oral activity for assessment (group interaction – discuss, argue, persuade):

a In a group, choose one topic about which you have a variety of views – the need for qualifications, your local football team, school dinners, etc.

b Each comment on the topic briefly, giving both your opinion and your reasons for it.

c Talk about the ways in which opinions are formed (for instance, 'I have always loved Hartley United since my grandad took me to my first match when I was four').

d Discuss whether differences of opinion are a good or a bad thing – or just an unavoidable part of life.

During reading

1 **a** As you read the extracts in this section, look at four things – the readership the writer or writers are addressing, the topic they are commenting on, the opinion they are expressing and the ways in which they express it.

b While reading or just after, jot down a few notes on each of those four areas – readership, topic, opinion, technique.

2 When you have finished making your notes, share them with a partner or in a small group, and discuss what, in your view, makes an effective piece of written commentary.

After reading

Select a question from *either* the linked writing *or* the coursework questions at the end of this book and follow the instructions to help you prepare and answer the question.

Section 3

Writing to argue, persuade, advise

Argument, persuasion and advice all have one thing in common – the writer has a clear point of view which they are trying to get across: because they want you to agree with them, when they are arguing a case; because they want you to behave in a particular way, when they are trying to persuade you; or because they want to tell you how best to go about something, when they are seeking to advise. The definitions below may help you to get the characteristics of each kind of writing clear in your mind.

Writing to argue: All the texts in this section are written by people with a very clear point of view about a particular topic, be it pacifism, supermarkets or romance, and in these texts they are arguing their case. As you read, look out for the ways in which the writers emphasise the aspects of the topic which they want their reader to agree with, by using vivid and occasionally very emotional language.

Writing to persuade: The texts in this section all have one thing in mind – to persuade you of a point of view, and to encourage you to take a particular kind of action, from helping the homeless to travelling to Myanmar (Burma). Persuasion is a step further than argument – you're not just arguing a case, you're using every tool at your disposal to get your readers to do what you want.

Writing to advise: All the texts in this section are written in order to advise their readers on a certain course of action or behaviour. Unlike argument, where the writer's viewpoint is the most important element, or persuasion, where the reader's response is the most important, in advice both reader and writer are assumed to share a common interest – the writer has expert knowledge which he or she shares with the reader in order to help them.

Writing to argue

Extract 3.1: 'Oxford for Peace'

The letter below is taken from the website of a movement called 'Oxford for Peace'. It was written and sent to the then Prime Minister, Tony Blair, less than a month after the destruction of the Twin Towers in New York, arguing that Britain's role in the military strikes against Afghanistan was against Tony Blair's own declared aims and beliefs, and that there were much more constructive actions he should have taken.

Oxford for *Peace*

Rt Hon Tony Blair MP   Oxford for Peace
10 Downing Street   43 St Giles
London SW1 0AA   Oxford

7 October 2001

Dear Tony Blair

Oxford for Peace calls for all violence and hostilities in Afghanistan to cease immediately. We believe that the military strikes begun today in response to the terrorist attack of 11 September 2001 will prove to be counterproductive to true peace and security.

Enclosed is the Oxford Petition for Peace which has more than 1700 signatures. Together with the tens of thousands of voices across the country, we call for a non-violent response to the crisis in which we now find ourselves.

People in Oxford of all backgrounds and ages urge you to uphold peace and a process of justice to effectively address the underlying causes of international terrorism. This includes measures to strengthen the role of the UN in extraditing and putting on trial suspected terrorists. We believe that true security will come from international co-operation based on equality, justice and the rule of law and the resolution of conflict through peaceful means.

We would like to quote words you spoke at the Labour Party Conference in Brighton, 2001, which we hope have not been completely undermined by the airstrikes on Kabul. It is urgent you put these words into action. On behalf of those who have signed the Oxford Petition for Peace, we urge you:

ACTION ONE: You spoke of 'a new beginning where we seek to resolve differences in a calm and ordered way'. Now is the time to show personal leadership by convincing our American allies that the International Criminal Court should and can play an effective and pivotal role in promoting global justice, adhering always to the principle of innocent until proven guilty.

ACTION TWO: You said 'if we wanted to, we could breathe new life into the Middle East Peace Process and we must.' Now is the time to show personal leadership by immediately calling for a Middle East Peace Process that brings peace, equality, sustainable development and new hope to the whole region.

ACTION THREE: You stated 'equality is about equal worth, not equal outcomes'. We are hearing a very different message in Oxford, especially from the young who signed the Oxford Petition for Peace. Equality for them is about equal outcomes on a global scale. The low turnout from the young at the last General Election is a shocking indictment on the current state of our democracy. Now is the time to listen especially to the young who are our future and want peace and rethink what equality means.

Oxford for Peace invites you to come and meet young people from our community who have signed our petition and listen to their views on peace, justice, equity and equality. Our hope is, as you stated in your speech 'out of the shadow of this evil, should emerge lasting good' and that more mistakes involving violence and military might are not repeated.

Yours for peace and justice, equity and equality

(signed)

Enclosures: Oxford Petition for Peace; video 'Non-violence for a change', Quaker Peace and Social Witness Programme; press coverage of Oxford for Peace procession on 22 September 2001

Extract 3.2: 'Supermarkets are bad for your health' by James Millar

This text comes from a magazine called *The Grocer*, which is aimed at those working in the food retail trade. In this article, James Millar, who founded and runs an independent grocery home shopping company, argues against the dominance of the big supermarkets.

James Millar argues that consumers' reliance on convenience food is dangerous because it eats away at our individual sense of responsibility.

A recent survey has just pronounced my local town, Tetbury, the third most desirable place to live in the UK. Tetbury, undeniably, is a nice place to live. Yet the only places you can buy apples, cauliflowers or a bag of potatoes are the local Somerfield and the almighty new Tesco. The fruit and vegetable shops have gone – shut down. We have two local butchers' shops and I wouldn't count their chickens.

Supermarket proliferation is unbounded, tethered only by conscientious objectors. Once majestic on their awesome out of town sites, they have marched relentlessly deeper and deeper into our cities, towns, villages and now, with Tesco's recent convenience store move, even onto the borough high street – surely the last preserve of the local shop. They are simply everywhere: garage forecourts, stations, boutique sites in the City, in your drive.

In a world of increasing freedom of choice, the British shopper is entitled to vote with his feet and travel to the local supermarket if he wishes. Competition is a wonderful thing and nowhere does it show itself more clearly than in supermarket retail figures. This is not my point. I simply question the social wisdom, the engineering and the societal consequences of allowing these modern monopolies even greater bites of the cherry.

Food shopping is an intensely personal matter; one is what one eats. Our nation is getting fatter and less healthy. Fewer and fewer people cook. Microwaves are installed – not ovens. Eating out is preferred to making something at home. People are taking the easy option and are being strongly encouraged to do this by the supermarket regime. Through the way supermarkets work, our connection with real food is gently being sucked away.

Supermarkets are designed for speed and efficiency. They are not designed for human interface. They are certainly not designed for exactly the sort of personal exchange that the local shopkeeper indulged in. They are de-humanised. In a supermarket, there is no one knowledgeable to turn to; no one is on hand to advise which bit is best to cook; no one provides a handy tip on seasonality. There is no one to have a good natter with. And the direct result of this is a loss of knowledge, a loss of understanding about food, a loss of connectivity with the very stuff we went in to buy.

It may all be there, written in mini letters in six different languages or covered in blood on the inside of the label. But it's not the same; it's not convincing; it's not a human being who means it. Instead we probably won't be cooking the casserole at all; we'll go for the easier microwave option because we're not sure how long to grill a mackerel; we'll forego making the fresh tomato salad because we're not sure of the quantities. We certainly won't be making marmalade this winter, because there's so much choice at the supermarket.

This is a dangerous tactic. It is another notch cut in the stick that measures our individual responsibility. We can become too reliant on the commercial orders of large corporates.

Lord Haskins argued for more supermarkets. I argue the exact opposite. We need a better balance on the high street between supermarket and local shop; bring back the people element to food shopping; incentivise the knowledgeable shopkeeper to spread his advice; bring back local expertise; bring back interest in food. Restrict supermarket planning to where existing shops can still survive. They are a vital piece of the jigsaw – and we will all be the poorer for their continued demise.

Extract 3.3: 'Mother's Little Helpers' by Meredith F. Small

In the passage below from the popular science magazine *New Scientist*, Meredith F. Small argues that there are very particular and important reasons why humans have a longer childhood than any other animal on the earth.

It's official, our kids really do take an incredibly long time to grow up. Meredith F. Small wonders whether an evolutionary trick designed to help the family out has backfired on today's parents.

What is it about humans that makes us such late developers? Chimps are ready to reproduce by the age of eight, yet human childhood lasts twice as long as it should for an ape of our size and rate of growth. We spend more time as children than any other animal on Earth. And we alone continue to feed our offspring well into adolescence. It takes an estimated 13 million calories to bring up a child – a huge investment on the part of parents. And that's not to mention all the GameBoys and tickets to Disneyland. Why do we do it?

The puzzle of childhood has intrigued researchers for decades. Some believe that a long childhood is simply a by-product of our long lifespan and requires no special explanation. But many anthropologists are convinced there must be some evolutionary advantage to prolonged immaturity. Humans live complicated lives: we have culture, language and technical skills enabling us to migrate across the globe and prosper. We can build cities and civilisations, and survive on our wits and intellect. Perhaps our childhood is so different because we have so much more to learn than other animals? Or perhaps, as one anthropologist now claims, long childhoods evolved to benefit parents, not kids. He believes it's only now, in the developed world at least, that childrearing has become so costly.

One possible clue to the extended childhood enigma is found by looking at when it evolved. Interestingly, the appearance of a long childhood coincides with a rapid increase in human brain size. Could the two be connected? It can't simply be about giving our big brains longer to grow because they stop growing way before adulthood. But perhaps it provides the time required for rewiring the hardware to help us cope in the adult world?

Hillard Kaplan from the University of New Mexico, Albuquerque, argues that we need a prolonged childhood to learn how to survive our complex adulthood. During this time of fewer responsibilities, he says, children have the space and freedom to acquire the skills and technical knowledge that will serve them as adults when no one is watching or helping. Those skills could mean the difference between life and death. Quite simply, childhood is an investment in the future.

It's an appealing idea because it fits with modern notions of childhood, where kids spend time in school, studying and acquiring skills to help them function effectively as adults. But there is little direct evidence to support it and other anthropologists protest that learning is not the point of childhood, and never was. New findings support their view that kids are actually quite proficient in survival skills, at least as hunters and gatherers. If childhood has become a time of learning today, these researchers argue, that's simply modern culture taking advantage of an extended life cycle stage that is already in place for other reasons.

Earlier this year, Nicholas Blurton-Jones from UCLA and Frank Marlowe from Harvard University published results from their studies of Hadza people from northern Tanzania (*Human Nature*, vol. 13, p. 199). The Hadza are primarily hunters and gatherers, but some children also attend boarding school where they sit at desks all day. Would time spent away at school affect the children's bush skills? Blurton-Jones and Marlowe devised a series of contests to discover. They found that young men who had been practising all their lives were no better at using a bow and arrow or climbing baobab trees to collect honey than those who had been away at school. Although hunting skills, in particular, varied among individuals, childhood experience had almost no effect on who became the best hunters. In fact, hunting efficiency peaks at around 40, so adult experience is probably more significant.

If childhood for modern hunter-gatherers is not about learning or refining adult skills, then our ancestors probably didn't need childhood for extensive learning either. 'There *is* a lot for foragers to learn,' comment Blurton-Jones and Marlowe in their paper. 'But does it really take so much time to learn it? Perhaps it would if we learned mostly by trial and error, like a rat or a pigeon in the laboratory. But from an early age, humans imitate and get instruction, and hear people talking about work. Human learning is very rapid. Even small children are rapid and capable learners.'

Other new research by Rebecca Biege Bird and Douglas Bird from the University of Maine also suggested that childhood is more about growing into complex tasks than learning them (*Human Nature*, vol. 13, p. 239). Observing Meriam children and adults of the Torres Strait, Australia, as they gathered shellfish or fished with lines and spears, the Birds discovered that children were just as good as adults at both line fishing and spear fishing, tasks that are technically difficult and require a lot of know-how about fish, tides and bait. But strangely, kids were not as good as adults at gathering shellfish, a job that anyone can do by simply bending over and grabbing. 'Shellfish collecting on Mer involves lots of walking to search for tridacnid clams and conch that are thinly dispersed across the mid-littoral of the reef,' says Bird. 'So if you walk faster, your encounter rate for highly profitable prey types will increase.' But once the kids were older and larger, more efficient walkers and less often distracted, they made competent gatherers.

The point is that kids grow into the task simply through physical development, not through learning or practice. The children were great at fishing although fishing takes almost adult cleverness to figure out, and they were held back at gathering only because they were smaller and less able than adults. 'It doesn't take the whole length of the human childhood to learn even complex foraging tasks,' says Biege Bird. 'Size and strength often trump experience.'

If childhood isn't about learning to feed yourself, is it about acquiring the social skills humans are so good at? 'Understanding the complexities of social interactions takes many years with many opportunities for social engagement, social interaction and social reasoning about experiences,' says developmental psychologist Melanie Killen of the University of Maryland. But recent research suggests that children know more about social relations than we give them credit for, and they learn the ropes early. Even babies will start to cry when they hear other babies in distress, which suggests a degree of empathy, fundamental for all positive human social behaviour. Children as young as four have a sense of fairness, according to studies done by William Damon of Stanford University. And Killen's own work with preschool children indicates that they use this, as well as remarkably well-developed negotiation skills, in their everyday dealings with one another.

If a long childhood isn't designed to give kids time to learn, then what is it for? Anthropologist Barry Bogin of the University of Michigan-Dearborn has proposed a radical alternative. Bogin argues that early childhood – between about age three to seven in modern humans – is a new phase inserted into the life cycle of our ancestors to increase reproductive success. He points out that all other mammals continue suckling their young until their permanent molars have erupted and they can fend for themselves. This limits the number of offspring each mother can produce. Bogin's idea is that our prolonged childhood is the result of evolution favouring this new life cycle phase where infants are no longer totally dependent on their mothers, but can rely on other family members for food and help. This means mothers can become pregnant again even though they still have small children.

The simple fact that humans are a highly successful species supports Bogin's idea. Despite our size, our long generation lengths and our long lives, we breed at the rate and with the success of small mammals with short lives. The typical interval between children is two and a half years, compared with five years for chimps, for example. More significantly, about twice as many human babies reach the age of fifteen than do chimp babies.

What's more, the idea of kids as 'dependent' is a modern concept that clouds our understanding of what it really means to be a child. In many parts of the world children contribute significantly to the household and are not really burdens. Across the globe, children typically look after their younger siblings and do household chores such as gathering firewood, weeding fields and tending livestock. And they do all this while still small and not competing much for resources such as food and household space. For parents in these cultures, childhood may be too short rather than too long.

Of course, for many families these days the tables have turned. Children may have evolved as 'little helpers' but in the developed world, at least, they have become a drain on household energy and income. If parents originally benefited from an extended childhood, kids have the upper hand now. We feel compelled to keep providing for our offspring even well after they reach sexual maturity. Paying for a good education makes perfect sense as an investment for our kids' future – even if it means they don't become independent until well into their twenties. And so what if they demand cash for new computer games, the movies or a holiday? Childhood, we tell ourselves, is special. Even if, occasionally, we wonder why it has to be so long.

Extract 3.4: 'In Defence of Romance' by Alan Loy McGinnis

The following text comes from a book entitled *The Romance Factor: How to Fall in Love ... and Stay in Love*. Here the writer argues that there are particular skills which are needed in order to keep a relationship alive. He uses a bank of quotations from other writers before he presents his ideas – why do you think he does that?

In the relation of a man and a woman who love each other with passion and imagination and tenderness, there is something of inestimable value, to be ignorant of which is a great misfortune to any human being.

Bertrand Russell

There is no surprise more magical than the surprise of being loved. It is the finger of God on a man's shoulder.

Margaret Kennedy

Americans, who make more of marrying for love than any people, also break up more of their marriages ... But the figure reflects not so much failure of love as the determination of people not to live without it.

Morton Hunt

My chief occupation, despite appearances, has always been love. I have a romantic soul, and have always had trouble interesting it in something else.

Albert Camus

When my first marriage ended and the news began to leak out, I felt very foolish entering the pulpit each Sunday. If I could not hold my own family together, what possible counsel could I offer to others? Like most pastors, I was often called on to help couples with marital problems, and continuing that seemed the height of hypocrisy.

Late one night a parishioner called and needed to talk. I met him at the church office, and he began to tell how his marriage was on the rocks. He obviously did not know about my divorce.

'Wait a minute,' I said. 'There's something I've got to tell you about myself.' I went on to explain the situation and said, 'If you want the names of other counsellors, I'll be glad to refer you to someone.'

He reflected a moment, then replied, 'No, I think I'd like to talk to you. My cardiologist had a heart attack last year too, but I still go to him.'

To my astonishment, I found myself doing more counselling than ever, perhaps because victims of similar coronaries have something in common. Or perhaps because people want to hear from others who have learned some things the hard way.

The more I thought about my own failed love and the more troubled people I saw (counselling eventually became my full-time occupation), the more I realised that I still had everything to learn about romance and love. I needed to have answers to questions such as the following:

- Can old-fashioned romantic love work in this age of one-night stands and quick divorce?
- What *is* that initial rush of elation that causes two people to stay up all night talking? Is it a feeling? A force? A decision?

- Can you get the feeling back once you've fallen out of love?
- And why does romance die? Is it possible to hate someone you once loved? Or could it be that you never actually loved that person in the first place?

To answer these queries, I read hundreds of books and articles by experts in the field and talked to dozens of scholars. After all the research, I'm still an incurable romantic. Some people view romance as a great mystery, something that happens to them beyond their control, as if falling in love were like falling in a pond. But, as Erich Fromm says, the word *falling* in the phrase 'falling in love' is a contradiction in terms. To 'fall' denotes passivity, and love is the most active of occupations.

You can generate love

William Lederer, who writes extensively on love and marriage, says, 'Love is not the cause of good relationships, it is the consequence of good relationships.' This is a very important point. Ordinarily, we think love must come first, and only then do we set about forming relationships. But Lederer says that it works the other way. An initial attraction may get things started, but *the quality of the relationship determines the emotions generated*.

A good example of the generation of love is the meeting of actor Robert Redford and Lola Van Wagenen. She was just out of high school, and he had returned from a lonely trip in Italy, where, he says, he had started drinking heavily and had begun to feel like 'an old man'.

'Lola's attitude,' he says in retrospect, 'was so fresh and responsive. I had so much to say to her that I started talking, sometimes all night long. She was genuinely interested in what I had to say, at a time when I really needed to talk. There were nights when we would walk down Hollywood Boulevard to Sunset, then up Sunset to the top of the hills, then over to the Hollywood Bowl and back to watch the dawn come up – and we'd still be talking. I had always said I'd never get married before I was thirty-five, but my instincts told me that this was a person I'd like to go through life with.'

Later Redford found himself in New York, missing Lola. He called her from a pay phone, and said, 'I have $32 in quarters. Let's decide whether we're going to get married or not.'

Lola knew how to fan initial interest into a flame. Instead of waiting for love to 'happen', she created a relationship, and love was the natural result. They have been married since 1958.

So love is not a fiat from Cupid's bow, it is something you create. And when you have learned to create it, you have mastered one of the most important skills we can ever learn.

Extract 3.5: 'From Crisis to Coping'

The following text comes from a book, *Adolescence: From Crisis to Coping*, edited by Janice Gibson-Cline. The authors look at the ways in which young people in a range of different countries deal with difficult social conditions. Here they argue that things are not nearly as clear-cut as they seem, and that even the most disadvantaged children find ways of coping.

Traditional theories of adolescence describe this stage of life as one of crisis and are often construed to imply that it is the stage of adolescence that generates these crises. To the contrary, while our subjects provided many indications of involvement in crises, with few exceptions, these were rooted in the external situations in which these youngsters found themselves, rather than in their own internal psyches.

It is sad that adolescents admitted abusing themselves with drugs or alcohol or with attempted suicide. While this behaviour contributes to problems, it is important that these youngsters reported it as a problem rather than as a solution. A systems-theory approach would suggest that this is a first step toward a productive solution.

Some coping responses reported by our subjects may be construed as non-productive, at least in terms of bettering their long-term situations. Examples include coping by disengaging, giving up or resigning themselves to their situations, although, in some cases, these views reflected realistic views of their options.

'I realise there isn't much I can really do, so I try not to think about it.' (Australia)
'When I worry about school, I go listen to music or stay alone at home.' (Israeli Arab)

'Sometimes when I do badly, I make myself feel better by telling myself that I am at least smarter than *some* people.' (Continental US)

The only subjects to report antisocial hostile-aggressive behaviour directed at their offenders were Russian males and immigrant males in the Netherlands. Both groups were dealing with political problems out of their control.

What external crises generate problems for adolescents? We suggest that, throughout the countries we studied, from the People's Republic of China to Kuwait, educational systems are in crisis and unable to provide adequate learning environments to teach skills needed by many students.

Family institutions are also in crisis and increasingly ill-equipped to provide children with needed support.

'My parents don't give me freedom.' (India)

'I'm so worried about my mother. She has been ill and doesn't take care of herself.' (Netherlands)

'My father went away. My mother cleans houses, but she cannot find a good job. I worry that we will not be able to go to school.' (Venezuela)

Governmental and political crises stemming from ills that range from economic problems to corruption increase the problem.

'Entrance examinations to university are not fair and I'm afraid I won't have a chance to get a good education.' (Soviet Russia)

Venezuelan and Brazilian subjects worried about street violence, and Arab Israelis about 'catastrophes'.

We suggest that adolescents, although particularly vulnerable to all of these external crises at their stage of life, are capable of coping actively and using resources available to them in effective ways – so long as they are helped to understand their situations and are given appropriate support by the adult world. When Sultana, the Greek Gypsy girl, understands that the causes for her lack of money are more complex than the fact that people 'don't buy flowers as they used to', she may be more likely than now to explore new coping strategies. So long as her poverty narrows her view of the causative factors related to her impoverished condition, however, she is not likely to search for more daring solutions than to 'sit down with the children and start singing'.

For those youngsters whose problems are related to drug or alcohol abuse – an increasing world plague – the first step, similarly, is understanding the cause of the problem. Appropriate counselling *can* help.

Writing to argue: Activities

Before reading – oral activities

1 Oral activity for access:

In a pair or in a small group, choose a topic about which you have strong views – for instance, animal experiments, student fees, blood sports, genetic engineering.

a Briefly sum up the arguments *on both sides* of your chosen topic.

b Try and suggest evidence which could back up each argument.

c Discuss how you would present your views.

2 Oral activity for assessment (drama-focused activity – discuss, argue, persuade):

a In a group of four, imagine that you are a family group – mother, father and two teenage children. Choose a scenario (staying out late, going on holiday, going to a gig, etc.) in which a difference of opinion between parents and children could arise.

b Divide into two – parents in one pair, teenagers in the other, and brainstorm all the reasons for your point of view.

c When each pair has sorted out their arguments, act out a scene round the family breakfast table in which each member of the family puts forward their views. Make it an exchange of points of view – not a slanging match!

d If you like, you could act out your scene in front of the class, and get them to vote on which argument was most convincing.

During reading

A written argument is not just somebody banging the table and saying, 'This is what I think!' It is a presentation of a series of views, some of which the writer agrees with, and some of which they wish to question.

1   As you read the extracts in this section, look at the ways in which the writer or writers develop their arguments, and how they include and discuss opposing views. Look, too, at the way they use evidence to back up their views, and how they structure their arguments so that the views they agree with come out on top.

2   While you are reading or just after you have finished, make brief notes under five headings:

   • topic
   • arguments for
   • arguments against
   • evidence
   • technique (e.g. structure, comparisons, rhetorical questions).

   Use references to and short quotations from the text to pinpoint your remarks.

After reading

Select a question from *either* the linked writing *or* the coursework questions at the end of this book and follow the instructions to help you prepare and answer the question.

Writing to persuade

Extract 3.6: 'Why Cry?'

This advertisement, which appeared in *Junior* magazine, a publication aimed at parents and carers of young children, is trying to sell a new kind of baby monitor, which does not only pick up the baby's cries, but also 'translates' them. Who do you think the target market is, and how does the advertisement try to appeal to them?

Why Cry?

When your baby cries, do you know why?

Babies cry for the same reason adults talk, to communicate their needs. Babies may cry because they are hungry, hot, cold, or just because they want to feel a little more secure.

Sometimes it is difficult to know exactly what your baby does need, especially if you are a first-time parent and are not yet in tune to your baby's cries.

As time goes by, first-time parents learn to identify the reason why their babies are crying, but until then they can only rely upon trial-and-error to assess exactly what it is that their baby needs.

Aware of the great importance all parents place upon their children's well-being, and being parents themselves, the developers at WhyCry® have created an electronic device that analyses your baby's cries and SHOWS YOU THE REASON FOR IT!

The WhyCry® Monitor has been clinically tested in Europe, with a success rate of 98 per cent when used in conjunction with the accompanying symptoms chart.

For further information please telephone 0207 36328. Or visit www.why-cry.co.uk

Extract 3.7: 'Loving Yourself' by Cherie Carter-Scott

This passage comes from a book called *If Love is a Game, These are the Rules*. Here the author is seeking to persuade her readers that self-esteem is the most important element in any successful relationship.

Your relationship with yourself is the central template from which all others are formed. Loving yourself is a prerequisite to creating a successful and authentic union with another.

The relationship you have with yourself is the central relationship in your life. At the heart of all the elements that make up your life experience – family, friends, love relationships, work – is you. This is why a book about the rules of love begins with a rule not about relationships with others, but rather about the one you have with yourself.

There is a distinction between 'you' and your 'self'. Your self is the core of your being, the essential entity that exists irrespective of your personality, your ego, your opinions and your emotions. It is the small, sacred space within you that houses your spirit and soul. 'You' are the observer, coach, editor and critic who surveys your thoughts, words, feelings and behaviours and determines how much of your essential self is shown to others.

The quality of the relationship between you and your self is paramount, for all your other relationships are based on it. This relationship acts as a template from which all the unions in your life are shaped, setting the quality, tone and texture for how you relate to others and how they relate to you. It establishes the working model of how to give and receive love.

The depth and quality of the link between you and your self ultimately determines the success of your relationships with others. If an authentic love relationship is what you desire, then the first natural step you must take is to learn to love, honour and cherish yourself as a truly precious and lovable being.

The Missing Puzzle Piece

Thousands of people have come to my personal growth workshops over the years to determine how they can find the love relationships they seek. I usually start by asking them to describe in detail how this person they seek would treat them, how they would feel around this partner and how they would ideally want to relate. The responses, of course, vary from person to person, but several constants always surface: most say they want someone who is kind, considerate and loving; who will treat them with respect and unconditional acceptance and listen to their wishes, goals and dreams; who will make them feel special and cherished; who will cheer at their successes; someone with whom they can be open and honest and to whom they can feel completely connected in heart, mind, body and soul.

When I ask these same people how many of these behaviours and actions they extend to themselves, most sheepishly admit that the answer is little to none. Many will acknowledge that they are critical of their flaws, override many of their needs, take for granted their positive attributes and accomplishments, and generally devote little time or attention to connecting with their own hearts and spirits. The same people who are seeking true love have little idea of how to offer it to themselves.

The place within you that generates self-love is the exact same place that attracts authentic love from others. If that source is clouded, your ability to attract a relationship that glistens with the magical sparkle of love is eclipsed. In order to bring light to that inner source, you will need first to learn how to give to yourself what you are seeking from another. Love creates more love, and when your own inner love light shines, you open yourself to experience the beautiful wonder of a deep and powerful connection with another being.

Extract 3.8: 'Work This Out'

Overleaf is an advertisement which appeared in *The Big Issue*, a magazine founded to help homeless people earn money so that they can begin to rebuild their lives. How effective do you think the language and layout are in catching your attention and making you think about the issues which are discussed?

ARE YOU MAD? SEE THOSE HUDDLED FIGURES? THEY'RE PEOPLE. WE MAY NOT BE SUFFERING HALLUCINATIONS OURSELVES, BUT WE DO SEEM TO BE ABLE TO WIPE SIGNIFICANT OBJECTS ENTIRELY FROM OUR VISUAL FIELD. IT SEEMS MANY OF US DON'T CONSIDER HOMELESS PEOPLE TO BE SIGNIFICANT OBJECTS. MAYBE WE'VE DEVELOPED SOME FORM OF HOMELESS-PHOBIA. RECOGNISE ANY OF THESE SYMPTOMS? IRRITATION, ANXIOUSNESS, INABILITY TO EMPATHISE, EVEN PARANOIA – WHERE YOU IMAGINE HOMELESS PEOPLE HAVE SCREWED THEIR LIVES UP, LOST THEIR LOVED ONES, AND GIVEN UP ALL THEIR WORLDLY POSSESSIONS IN ORDER TO TAKE YOU FOR A RIDE. DOESN'T THAT QUALIFY AS DELUSIONAL? IF IT'S NOT QUITE CLASSIFIABLE BEHAVIOUR, IT CERTAINLY HIGHLIGHTS AN IMBALANCE IN REASONING. HERE'S ANOTHER. THERE ARE LESS THAN A THOUSAND OFFICIAL ROUGH SLEEPERS IN GREAT BRITAIN'S MAJOR CITIES. NOTHING COMPARED TO THE FIFTY-SIX MILLION MORE FORTUNATE INDIVIDUALS WHO IGNORE THEM EVERY DAY. EVEN WHEN YOU ADD THOSE IN HOUSEHOLDS REGARDED AS TEMPORARY ACCOMMODATION (INCLUDING BED AND BREAKFAST, HOSTELS, OVERNIGHT SHELTERS AND MISSIONS), IT'S STILL A GREAT DEAL LESS THAN ONE PERCENT OF OUR TOTAL POPULATION. THE TRUTH IS THERE ARE FAR MORE PEOPLE SUFFERING FROM HOMELESSNESS IN THIS COUNTRY THAN THERE ARE HOMELESS PEOPLE. WE JUST NEED TO ADMIT IT TO OURSELVES. THAT'S WHEN THE BIG ISSUE CAN HELP. WE PROVIDE SUPPORT FOR MENTAL ILLNESS, ADDICTION, SEXUAL ABUSE, TRAINING, EDUCATION AND RE-ACCOMMODATION. A SOURCE OF HOPE BOTH FOR THE HOMELESS AND THOSE WITH A PROBLEM WITH THE HOMELESS. IT'S SAID THAT IN CONFRONTING ANY PROBLEM THE FIRST STEP IS THE HARDEST. SO TAKE HEART. THE FACT THAT YOU'RE STILL READING IS STEP ONE. THE BIG ISSUE FOUNDATION. **THINK BIGGER**.

**WORK THIS OUT.
A PERSON DIAGNOSED
WITH A MENTAL DISORDER
SLEEPS IN A DOORWAY.
A PERSON WHO'S
COMPLETELY SANE
WALKS RIGHT PAST THEM
EVERY MORNING.**

Extract 3.9: 'Animal Circuses – Animal Suffering'

The text below is a leaflet on animal circuses, put out by a campaigning organisation, the Captive Animals' Protection Society, to persuade you to help them with time or money to put an end to what they argue is animal suffering. The leaflet uses facts, photos and anecdotes to put across its point of view. Which do you find most persuasive?

It is hard to believe that circuses still tour the UK with performing animals. The Circus Friends Association lists ten touring circuses with animals. There are also two static animal circuses. The animals touring include elephants, a bear, lions, tigers, snakes, camels, llamas, goats, horses, ponies, ducks, pigeons, cats and dogs. Circuses may lease animal acts, so the line up can change from year to year.

Don't go to circuses with animal acts!

By their very nature, circuses cannot provide the space and stimulation that animals need. Continuity of veterinary treatment may become a problem, as well as getting a regular and varied food supply. Animals suffer physically and mentally in the circus.

What do we learn?

There is no educational value in seeing these once proud animals reduced to performing tricks in an unnatural environment. What can we learn about the majestic elephant, sitting on a tub whilst surrounded by bright lights and loud music? What do we learn about the endangered tiger, made to walk across a tightrope?

Tricks are certainly not an extension of wild behaviour. Elephants do not stand on their heads; bears do not walk on barrels; and baboons do not ride ponies. Circuses simply teach a lack of respect for animals.

Life on the road

Circus animals endure long periods of confinement, for hours, sometimes even days. For lions and tigers, home for the 'season' is a beast wagon – a cage on the back of a lorry. They may have occasional access to a small 'exercise' cage but this is usually so small that any exercise is negligible. Horses spend most of their days in small pens or tied on short ropes.

In the wild elephants may walk up to 70 kms (45 miles) per day. Circus elephants spend much of their time chained by their legs, barely able to move. It is impossible for circuses to provide appropriate facilities for such animals.

Circus animals are often kept in unnatural social groups. In the wild, elephants, zebras and camels will live in large groups or herds. Horses enjoy the company of their own kind, yet in a circus, these animals are often kept alone or in small groups.

Abnormal behaviour

Circus animals such as elephants, camels and horses may display stereotypic behaviours. These are mindless repetitive behaviours caused by stress, frustration and boredom. Such behaviour is also seen in zoos and factory farms. Animals will repeatedly pace, chew their cage bars or sway. With little to do, the animals go out of their minds.

Claims by circus staff that animals are stimulated by performances are incorrect. In fact, the same tricks are generally repeated for years.

Training – hidden suffering

Methods used to train animals are questionable – who could forget the scenes filmed undercover by Animal Defenders of Mary Chipperfield and her associates beating and abusing animals.

Trainers often use sticks, whips or goads, in the ring, spikes may be hidden with tassels. Even walking sticks with a nail in the end are used to 'encourage' elephants. The audience may be oblivious to the abuse of animals going on right in front of them.

In the book *Elephant Tramp*, former circus trainer George Lewis says 'We had only three weeks in which to get things into shape, and the elephants had not been worked for some time. Sadie and Elsie were the youngest of the eight, and were very timid. One day, when we had them in the ring barn urging them through one of their tricks, Sadie just could not grasp what we were trying to show her. In frustration she attempted to run out of the ring. We brought her back and began to punish her for being so stupid. We stopped suddenly and looked at each other, unable to speak. Sadie was crying like a human being. She lay there on her side, tears streaming down her face and sobs racking her body.'

Gene, another ex-circus employee, was interviewed by the US Elephant Alliance, 'She was a sweet little innocent brown bear who never hurt anyone. But sometimes she had trouble balancing on the high wire. She was then beaten with long metal rods until she was screaming and bloody. She became so neurotic that she would beat her head against her small cage. She finally died.'

In his book, *The Circus King*, Henry N. Ringling states 'It is not usually a pretty sight to see the big cats trained. All sorts of other brutalities are used to force them to obey the trainer and learn their tricks. They work from fear.'

Circus staff may allow visitors to see rehearsals. But these are simply animals being put through their paces – doing routines they may have done for years. The real training goes on behind closed doors.

When touring ends

When not on the road, circus animals live at their training or 'winter' quarters. Conditions here differ little to those touring. Animals may live permanently in their beast wagons, or in the case of elephants may be chained up in barns for days, weeks, even months.

How you can help end the circus misery

- Please, boycott circuses with animal acts, and urge others to do the same.
- Become a supporter of the Captive Animals' Protection Society (CAPS).
- Support non-animal circuses.
- Send an A4 stamped addressed envelope for our free information pack!
- Write to your local newspaper highlighting what is wrong with animal circuses, using information from this leaflet.
- Send a donation to help our campaign.

☐ I enclose a donation to help CAPS

☐ Please send me more information about CAPS

☐ I would like to become a CAPS supporter

Make cheques/POs payable to CAPS

Name: _____

Address: _____

Postcode: _____

**Captive Animals' Protection Society, PO Box 43, Dudley, DY3 2YP
www.caps-uk.dircon.co.uk**

Extract 3.10: 'Jobs in the Army'

The passage below comes from an Army Careers Guide, published by the army to persuade young people to join up – how do you think the text and picture work together to make becoming an infantry soldier attractive to the reader?

General George Patton once said: 'Wars may be fought with weapons, but they are won by men.' He wasn't wrong. The Army has the SA80 rifle, the AS90 self-propelled gun and the Challenger tank, but none of them are any use without one important item. The Mk1, standard issue, never-bettered British combat soldier.

But there's more to being a combat soldier than fighting. Combat units often have to use their skills to stop other people from fighting. In Kosovo, combat units have a been a key part of KFOR, NATO's peacekeeping force, and have had to do everything from patrolling the area and restoring its water supply to making sure that elections were fair.

The Infantry are one of the key parts of the Army's combat arm. Most of the 32 Infantry Regiments in the regular Army recruit in their own part of their country, but it doesn't always mean that they're local regiments for local people. Many will take recruits no matter where they're born, and three infantry regiments recruit on a national basis – the Foot Guards, the Royal Irish Regiment and the Parachute Regiment.

The Infantry wouldn't be effective without such regiments as the Household Cavalry, the Royal Armoured Corps and the Royal Artillery, a trio whose firepower and armour play a vital role on the battlefield. The Army Air Corps and the recently formed Attack Helicopter Team make the Army's battlefield capability even stronger, ensuring that combat soldiers don't always have to be earthbound.

WWW.ARMYCOMBAT.CO.UK

Extract 3.11: 'Myanmar Today'

The text which follows comes from the official Myanmar (Burma) government website. Its aim is to emphasise all the positive aspects of the country to persuade tourists to go and visit.

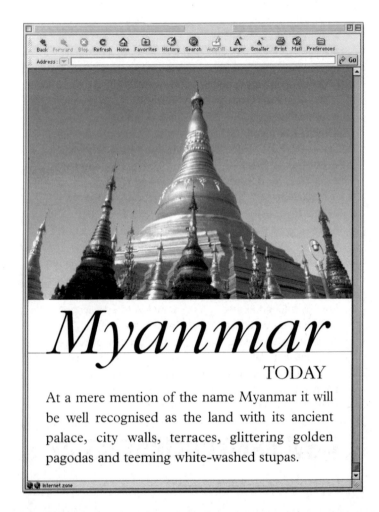

Myanmar
TODAY

At a mere mention of the name Myanmar it will be well recognised as the land with its ancient palace, city walls, terraces, glittering golden pagodas and teeming white-washed stupas.

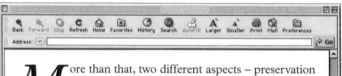

*M*ore than that, two different aspects – preservation of the beautiful natural environment, traditional customs and ancient cultural heritage on the one hand, and modern development on the other – constitute one of Myanmar's attractions.

As about half the total area of Myanmar is covered by forests, and Myanmar has been able to conserve the natural environment with its beauty rendered by rivers, creeks and streams, waterfalls, and its fauna and flora, it would not be wrong to call Myanmar a country of rare unspoilt natural beauty. Myanmar's evergreen forests yield valuable teak and other hardwoods. Just as Myanmar teak is world-famous, so also other woods such as Pyinkado, In, Kanyin and finished products are being exported to other countries.

Parallel with timber extraction from the forests, reforestation is being kept up systematically. Moreover, as conservation of the natural environment is maintained with priority consistently all along, a major project for the greening of the nine districts of the dry zone is being carried out. Now, one and all can enjoy the green and beautiful scenery around the area of Mount Popa of great renown. It has become a recreational resort for international tourism.

Gems of Myanmar are well known and widely liked in the world. Treasures from the gem mines of Myanmar have been famous since the days of the ancient Myanmar Kings. Since the thirteenth century, the best ruby has come from Mogok gemland. There is also produced sapphire of as great a quality as the ruby. Myanmar jade too is of world renown and highly popular. As thirty-six kinds of precious stones are being produced from the country, Myanmar is being praised as the land of gems.

Writing to persuade: Activities

Before reading – oral activities

1   Oral activity for access:

   a In a pair or in a small group, brainstorm a list of the advertisements which you have seen, heard or read in the last week, which you have found effective.

   b Select two or three advertisements from your list.

   c Talk about them in detail – how does each of them work? Do they have elements in common (for example, shock, humour, some kind of story)?

   d Discuss briefly which one you think was the most persuasive and why.

2   Oral activity for assessment (drama-focused activity – discuss, argue, persuade):

   a For this activity you will need three small groups. Imagine that each group represents an advertising agency. You have each been asked by a soft drinks manufacturer to put forward ideas for a television advertising campaign for a new soft drink aimed at the young teen market.

   b In your groups, brainstorm ideas for the advertising campaign. How will you persuade young teens (and their parents) to buy the product?

   c When each group has put together their ideas for a campaign, imagine that the rest of the class are executives working for the soft drinks manufacturer – you are going to need to persuade them that your advertising campaign is the best.

   d Each group in turn presents their advertising campaign and then, if you like, the class can vote on which one should get the commission.

During reading

As you read the extracts in this section, you need to keep in mind just what the purpose of persuasive writing is – persuasive writing is not just intended to get the reader to agree with you, but also to persuade them to take some course of action.

1 While you are reading, make brief notes on what the topic is that is being written about and what the writer wants to persuade you to do. Look at the techniques they are using (comparisons, varied sentence structure, graphics, etc.).

2 When you have finished reading, in a pair or in a small group, discuss how effective you think the passage was as a piece of persuasive writing, backing up your views with reference to or short quotations from the text.

After reading

Select a question from *either* the linked writing *or* the coursework questions at the end of this book and follow the instructions to help you prepare and answer the question.

Writing to advise

Extract 3.12: 'Are You Being Bullied?'

This text forms part of a school anti-bullying policy, and was displayed in classrooms and corridors, as well as being available for consultation by parents and teachers. The leaflet suggests a course of behaviour for students who are being bullied themselves or who see someone else being bullied.

Are You Being Bullied?

If you are being bullied the following responses should help.

- Talk to someone you can trust, e.g. best friend, teachers, form tutor.

- Try not to show you are upset.

- Try to ignore the bully.

- Walk quickly and confidently even if you don't feel that way inside.

- Try to be assertive – look and sound confident.

- If it is a group picking on you, walk quickly away.

- Avoid being alone in places where bullying takes place.

- If you are in danger get away.

You can help to stop bullying in the following ways.

- Don't stand by and watch – fetch help.

- Show that you and your friends disapprove.

- Give sympathy and support to other pupils who may be bullied. It could be your turn next.

- Be careful about teasing people or making personal remarks. If you think they might not find your comments funny then don't say them.

- If you know of serious bullying tell your form tutor. The victim may be too scared or lonely to tell.

Punishment for bullies

A The behaviour will be challenged and an incident slip completed by the form tutor.

B The form tutor will record incidents of bullying. Three incidents merit year tutor attention.

C The year tutor/assistant head of school will record incidents in a central 'bullying file'.

D Parents will be informed.

E School detention, if appropriate.

F Put on report.

G Senior manager involved.

H Temporary exclusion/internal suspension.

I Suspension.

Extract 3.13: 'Plastic Pollution: It's Everywhere!' by H. Steven Dashefsky

This text comes from a book of environmental science activities entitled *Kids Can Make a Difference*. Here the author advises his readers on ways of dealing with plastic pollution so as to avoid damage to wildlife and the environment.

Plastic Pollution: It's Everywhere!

You see it everywhere. Plastic wrappers, disposable lighters, foam cups, and packaging material are on the ground and in the water. Plastic pollution is a big problem in our cities and parks, on beaches, and even in the country.

Plastic should be thrown into trash containers, or it should be recycled, if possible. The truth is, however, that tons of plastic items are not recycled and are not put in the trash. They end up littering the land or floating in water. This plastic might come from people who carelessly litter, from sloppy garbage handling, from overflowing city sewer systems, or from people dumping it overboard from boats. Since plastics don't decompose quickly like natural products such as paper, they remain in our environment for a long time.

Plastic items don't remain where they fall. Plastic garbage makes its way into streams, rivers, and oceans by being washed into a storm drain, falling out of a beach garbage container, or being thrown overboard from a boat.

Plastic items can act like booby traps for many types of organisms. For example, turtles mistake plastic sandwich bags for jellyfish, eat them, and die from blocked intestines. Birds swallow bits of plastic foam and choke. Animals often become entangled in plastic debris such as fishing lines or plastic ropes and nets, and they either drown or starve.

When buying, using, and disposing of plastics, think about the harm they can cause to wildlife. Plastic is part of our everyday lives. As useful and important as it is, if not properly disposed of, it becomes a nuisance to us and a menace to wildlife.

Things you can do

You can do many things to help reduce plastic pollution. Try some of the following ideas and activities on your own or with friends and classmates.

- **Avoid buying products with plastic six-pack rings** (also called yokes). They are hard to see in the water and marine animals can get their heads or other parts of their bodies stuck in them. Since they cannot get themselves out, they often starve to death or are strangled. Don't litter the beach with them, since they are likely to be blown into the water. When you do use them, cut the rings before disposing of them. Organise a class plastic pollution clean-up day. See how many of these rings you find. What percentage of the litter you collected is plastic?

- **Don't release helium-filled balloons that float away**. These balloons are often used for celebrations in which they are released into the air as part of the festivities. Most people don't realise that these fun-filled floaters can kill marine life. They travel hundreds of miles from their release point and often end up in the ocean. The salt water washes off the dye, making them look clear, and many fish and marine animals mistake them for their favourite food – jellyfish.

These balloons can be eaten by whales, dolphins, sea turtles, seals, fish, and waterfowl. A balloon can become stuck in the food passage or stomach, preventing the animal from eating or digesting its food. The animal then starves to death.

The next time you hear about a party that plans to release balloons, contact the organisers and explain the problems that balloons can cause. Ask them to use alternatives. If balloons will be available at a celebration, find a way to inform people not to release them, even if you live hundreds of miles from the ocean. Ask parents to tie them to their children's clothing so they can't be lost accidentally.

Try using colourful wind socks or kites as alternatives when you have a party. Be sure to dispose of them properly when done.

Extract 3.14: *Mongolia: A Travel Survival Kit* by Robert Storey

The text below comes from a travel guide to Mongolia. Here the writer is trying to make it plain to the reader just what Mongolia is like, and what not to take for granted.

When to go
The travel season is from late May to early October, though Ulaan Baatar is feasible any time of year if you can tolerate the cold. From mid-October to mid-May, sudden snowstorms can ground flights, block roads and cause the transport system to break down completely.

June and September are both very pleasant times to visit the country. Early July gives you the best weather for the northern part of the country, though it will be stinking hot in the Gobi. July and August are the rainiest months, which makes jeep travel on dirt roads difficult. July is also the time to see the Naadam Festival. Unfortunately, this is also the peak tourist season, when Mongolia's inadequate accommodation and creaky transport is stretched to breaking point. To make matters worse, no work at all gets done during Naadam. In other words, expect everything (including restaurants) to be closed during the entire second week of July.

What to bring
Before deciding what to bring, decide what you are going to carry it in. A backpack is still the most popular form of luggage as it is convenient and the only choice if you have to do any walking. Rather than the 'open top' design, a backpack with zipped compartments is best. You can close the zips with some small padlocks to make the bag more thiefproof.

In most of these guidebooks, we tell you to 'bring as little as possible because you can and will buy things along the way'. However, this rule doesn't apply to Mongolia, where shortages of basic consumer goods are the norm. You should bring *everything* you need. If you can't fit it all into your backpack, pick up a cheap duffel bag (easy to do in China) and give the bag away when you leave Mongolia.

Food supplies are sketchy in Mongolia, so take some iron rations with you. There is an acute shortage of toilet paper, so come prepared. Hot water for making tea or coffee is seldom available, so an electrical immersion coil is essential for caffeine addicts, assuming you have the correct plug adaptor (see the Electricity section). You'll need an enamel cup for boiling the water, as plastic and glass are too fragile. Bring your own tea, coffee, coffee whitener and sugar if you need it (artificial sweetener packs better because it's smaller and won't attract bugs or rats). Curry powder adds flavour to Mongolia's bland diet of mutton and rice. A gluestick will ensure that your postage stamps remain stuck to the envelope or postcard, and sticky tape will prove to be worth its weight in gold – it can hold your maps together and can even be used to repair your jeep. Sunscreen (UV) lotion and sunglasses are indispensable. Plastic bags and twist ties will prove useful for storing bread, biscuits and dirty laundry. It's also a good idea to take along a few books.

If you want to give gifts to Mongolians, most would prefer something of practical rather than sentimental value. In rural areas, you can often barter these goods for petrol, rides on camels, a chance to take photos, etc. Some suggested gift items include chocolate, sweets, cigarettes, cigarette lighters, candles, vodka, rice, flour, noodles, pens and paper, T-shirts, socks, tea, coffee, toothpaste and sugar. Some of these items can be purchased in the dollar shops in Ulaan Baatar, so it isn't necessary to bring everything with you. Many Mongolians are trying to learn English and would appreciate some foreign magazines, books or newspapers. Warm clothes will be needed for any time of year, as even summer evenings can be chilly. Most Mongolians dress informally but you should avoid wearing revealing clothes, even on hot summer days.

A big decision is whether to bring a sleeping bag. Most visitors to Mongolia do not need one. The grand exceptions are when you're contemplating a jeep or camping trip. If camping, you need a sleeping bag. When travelling by jeep, you can usually stay in hotels, but when mechanical breakdowns occur (not uncommon) a sleeping bag can be a lifesaver. As a compromise, some travellers carry a so-called 'space blanket', a sheet of reflecting material which looks something like aluminium foil and folds up small enough to fit in your pocket. These are sold in backpacking shops and are intended to keep you alive in emergencies, but are no use at all for camping trips.

If you bring a camping stove, note that the easiest fuel to buy in Mongolia is petrol, followed by diesel. Kerosene is very scarce, and if you bring a stove which requires gas cartridges, you'll have to bring your own fuel. Gas cartridges should not, of course, be carried in planes.

Winter clothes
It is best to dress in layers. Silk and cotton are best for wearing next to the skin, followed by heavy cotton or wool shirts and then a sweater made from wool or some of the new artificial fibres. As long as temperatures remain below freezing (and therefore the air is dry), a goose down jacket is best for your outerwear, but down loses its insulating properties when wet. Your jacket

should have a hood attached to keep your head warm, but bring a stocking cap too. Don't forget the lower half of your body – long underwear will keep your bottom warm, and nylon windpants can be worn for extreme temperatures. On your feet, wear boots, preferably with some insulating fur on the inside. Mittens are warmer than gloves, but make sure they are well insulated. If you're going to be spending a lot of time outdoors in minus 50°C weather, you can also wear a special neoprene mask available from ski shops. Few people do so because it looks silly, but the mask will prevent your nose and cheeks from freezing. Sunglasses or goggles round out the outfit.

Extract 3.15: 'Beware of the Geese!' by Steve Chilcott

In this article, taken from a specialist magazine for people running smallholdings, the writer advises on the best kinds of fowl to raise for eggs to eat and sell. He tries to give insights into difficulties the reader might not have considered.

Beware of
the Geese!

In this article on setting up a smallholding, Steve Chilcott looks at getting geared up for production and admits that he has no fondness for the (alleged) defenders of ancient Rome.

Take a random sample of *Country Smallholding* back issues and you might be excused for thinking that the magazine is heavily poultry-orientated. Over a third of the cover photos in the last three years feature birds, principally chickens, and certainly adverts appearing in our local monthly smallholders' magazine are always predominantly bird-biased in subject matter.

That is because after the initial potato crop has been successfully lifted, or first crunchy lettuce cut, most would-be self-sufficiency types turn to the next most manageable enterprise, viz. poultry-keeping.

But you need to decide what you are keeping birds for, if that doesn't sound too much like teaching you to suck eggs! Do you want eggs, chicken-meat, rosettes at the local show or do you just want something animated to look at?

You're not running a zoo, so everything has to produce something of use. I've kept a range of poultry breeds purely for egg production over the years and after a recent flirtation with Light Sussex, Marans and Welsummers (I got bored temporarily with undistinguished brown chickens) I am back firmly in the hybrid camp.

Generally speaking, I buy in point-of-lay pullets in the spring, guaranteeing an egg supply throughout the summer and then sell off the majority after the October half-term (pretty much the end of the tourist year) by which time they are six months old and still 'in full profit'.

Geese

Geese are probably first choice for anyone with limited grass but with ambitions to expand into meat production.

Cobbett says that they are 'easily kept, live to a very great age and are amongst the hardiest animals in the world, and, if well kept ... will lay a hundred eggs in a year.' John Seymour calls them '... the most excellent birds for the self-supporter ... hardy, tough, self-reliant, and they make good mothers ...'.

I would love a fiver for everyone over the years who has told me they are 'excellent guard-dogs'. I can't imagine where that idea started! They are reputed to have saved ancient Rome from a surprise attack by hoards of hirsute Gauls by their vexatious cackling, but if truth be told, the guards on the city walls probably spotted them coming anyway and just got more irritated by the cacophony!

Geese will break out into nerve-jangling voice at pretty much any opportunity, day or night, and if you consider it always to be heralding an attack by ancient Gauls you will get precious little else done in the day!

Despite their apparent size and strength, geese are not very agile. If one attacks, you can immobilise it totally by grabbing it firmly round the neck if you have the bottle, and this, coupled with a lack of wit, makes them no match for the cunning fox who will attack from the rear and nip off their head.

Geese start to lay around St Valentine's Day (14 February – mine were always regular as clockwork) and as they have a pathetically short attention span, very rarely last the course, wandering off with a vacant look before the allotted month-long incubation period is up.

Better to buy a small incubator, put a cross or date-mark on one side and do the job by artificial means, turning and spraying daily.

Killing a goose is unpleasant and, when cooked, the quantity of edible meat is disappointingly small with a large amount of yellowy grease which was used in former times as hand cream, udder salve, poultice, waterproofer, butter substitute, leather softener, hoof polisher and even gout cure. Nowadays, it is an embarrassing by-product, difficult to dispose of.

Throughout the ages the main reason that geese were marched in huge droves with tarred feet, to be sold at Nottingham or Tavistock (Goosey Fair) was for their feathers, which were often plucked many times through the summer months, at six-week intervals, to be used as pillow or mattress stuffing, for making arrows for the feared and revered English longbows used at Crecy or Agincourt, and for quill writing implements, trimmed to a fine knib with a penknife.

The goose is the only creature I know that attacks you when you are feeding it or, if on free range, your visitors when they call round unexpectedly, which some find very frightening.

My geese also used to spend their leisure hours pecking out the putty on the patio doors, which infuriated me! I'm not keen on geese!

Extract 3.16: 'Give the GIFTS, Avoid the Gaffs' by Paul Coleman

In the passage below, from a book called *How to Say it for Couples*, Paul Coleman advises his readers on particular ways of behaving which will enable them to establish and maintain good relationships with their partners. He uses an acronym, GIFTS, to get his message across and to help his readers remember it. This is sometimes a useful strategy for helping your reader or listener follow your ideas – do you think it works here?

The GIFTS are perhaps *the most important tools* you can use to make your conversations both effective and gratifying. Without the GIFTS, your relationship will not be happy. With them, even couples with major issues to resolve stand a pretty good chance of overcoming them. I will mention them briefly now and point out the ways men and women differ in their use. Remembering to give the GIFTS (and avoid the *gaffs*) will transform difficult conversations into rewarding and intimate experiences.

• G Gentle

Try to begin discussions with a gentle touch. Keep your engines purring. (Roaring engines are a major gaff, especially at the outset of a conversation.) Anger is allowed but do your utmost to start the conversation less harshly. 'I'm angry and want to talk about this ...' is a gentler start-up than 'I can't believe you ignored my parents the entire night! Don't you know how rude that was?'

Men vs. Women: Research is clear that when it comes to making complaints, women are more likely to begin with their engines roaring instead of purring. (This is probably due to the fact that women can tolerate heightened emotions during discussions better than men can, and women anticipate men withdrawing from the discussion early – so their frustration shows right away.) Women must learn to start gently, and men must learn to hang in there when conversations get a bit intense.

• I In-flight repairs

Difficult conversations, by definition, can escalate into miserable arguments. 'Repair' comments such as 'I shouldn't have said that ... I'm feeling overwhelmed, can we take a break and talk again in twenty minutes? ... Please speak more softly ... I may not be right ... Can we begin again?' and others like them act as circuit-breakers that keep emotional energy from exploding.

Men vs. Women: Premature withdrawal from difficult conversations is a major gaff that most men make. Making in-flight repairs prevents that mistake. Repairs have a calming effect on both partners and enable men to have staying power.

• F Find hidden concerns

Many arguments are not what you are arguing about. Deeper issues of *Do you really love me? Am I important to you? Is this relationship fair?* can lie underneath. Ignoring these hidden issues is a gaff. Inquiring about such concerns may help you realise why your partner seems so irrationally upset about something that seems minor to you. He or she may really be upset about something unstated.

Men vs. Women: A woman is more intuitive and can therefore detect underlying issues. Usually a better listener, a woman makes eye contact more than a man and often senses subtle variations in tone and timing of speech. She detects apparent contradictions between the speaker's words and nonverbal language and may adamantly accuse that despite what the man actually said, she knows exactly what he meant. (Men hate it when that happens.)

• T Teamwork

If you must 'win' an argument, then the relationship loses and you have committed a major gaff. You are both on the same team, not adversaries. Unless you treat each other as such, nobody really wins. Teamwork implies a willingness to be influenced by your partner to some degree, to yield on certain points. No stubborn standoffs. Instead, find ways to say 'That makes sense ... I can understand why you feel that way ... I'll go along with that ...' Teamwork also means making time for one another during the day.

Men vs. Women: If someone is refusing to yield on certain points and has a hard time admitting that his partner's view has some merit, that someone is usually the man. Women are more willing to compromise for the sake of the relationship whereas some men regard being right as more important than being friends.

• S Supportive comments

Reassure your spouse that you love him or her. Appreciate what was done right, don't make a gaff by just criticising what you dislike. Let your partner know that you are proud of his or her accomplishments. If your partner is troubled or upset (especially if it's not about you), try to empathise.

Men vs. Women: A woman has tremendous power in this area. A man flourishes when he believes that his wife has faith in him and is proud of his accomplishments. Especially if he is going through a rough time personally, a wife who says 'I have faith in you' will boost his confidence (even if he initially scoffs at the remark). She doesn't necessarily need to help him explore his feelings. In fact, he might feel more vulnerable doing that. Men are supportive when they help a woman explore her feelings. Unfortunately, many men get to 'I'm sure it will all work out' as their attempt at support, and then try to change the subject.

Extract 3.17: 'Land Your Dream Job' by Mark Ramshaw

This text comes from *3D World*, a specialist magazine for those working, or hoping to work, in the 3D industry of computer graphics. Here readers are being advised on how to find the job that is just right for them.

Land Your Dream Job

Young, gifted and freelance? Or are you already working full-time, but looking to take that next step forward? Whatever your situation, our panel of experts will show you how to get your big break in the 3D industry.

Okay, so you got the education. Now what? A job where artistic muscles are stretched and 3D knowledge is utilised beckons. But where? 3D computer graphics pervade so many areas of media and business that choosing which area to specialise in is by no means easy. And how? Even if you know what career you'd like to pursue, there's still the mystery of how to make the leap from first job or lecture hall to major studio.

Part of the challenge facing graduates arises from the fact that 3D is so fantastically aspirational and yet undeniably specialised. There are precious few other areas of employment deemed so desirable and yet so reliant on extraordinary skill, and even armed with a degree, the job market is especially fierce. Getting your work seen by the right people is difficult. Obtaining an interview is a challenge. And actually getting the job is another matter altogether. To succeed, it's necessary to be aware of the quirks of each 3D field, and to appreciate exactly what employers are looking for – and what makes them choose one candidate over another.

Over the next few pages we've consulted those in the know – including experts from DreamWorks, The Mill and Electronic Arts – to give job seekers vital information about each major market sector. From whether cold calling is a good idea and what to put on that showreel when approaching a 3D ad design studio, to which qualifications are necessary for a job in Web graphics, it's all addressed here.

Industry experts reveal whether their particular field is in rude health or in recession, and what the ramifications are for potential employees. They also give vital advice on how to approach studios in the hope of bagging that elusive first job. The potential for building up experience doing freelance projects is covered, and in the case of the film and broadcast industries, the way contract work prevails over salaried positions is addressed.

We can't guarantee the tips, advice and comments here will win you a job in the industry, but they can certainly help you decide where to channel your energies and how best to sell yourself. They'll also let you know what your chances of success really are ...

Videogame animation

With the latest generation of superconsoles and sub-£1,000 PCs pumping high polygon counts into millions of living rooms, there's never been a better time to work as a games artist or animator.

The games market seems a world away from other industries reliant on 3D talent, not least because the bulk of the work involves designing for pared-down real-time rendering engines. Yet the modelling and texturing skills required are very similar to those used in film and broadcast, while the accelerated pace of the technology means that the disparity in lighting and effects is getting ever smaller. Furthermore, the industry offers graduates the potential to bag a permanent, relatively stable job. This isn't an industry reliant on freelance or contracting.

WORKING IN GAMES
Five Golden Rules

1 Look to the big studios
Larger companies are currently more stable, and also offer the best pay deals.

2 Do your research
If you hate modelling cars, don't apply to studios specialising in racing games.

3 Focus
Roles in the games industry are becoming more specific. Consider whether you want to focus on modelling, character animation or environment.

4 Visit shows
The games industry has its own shows, like GDC and ECTS. Visit these to make contact with studio heads and recruitment managers, rather than relying on agencies and cold calling.

5 Show you're a team player
Games are developed over a period of years by large teams, so personality is also a major consideration for employers.

Growing demand

Dominic Davenport at Escape Studios agrees. 'There is a growing demand for real artistic skill in the videogames industry. And new platforms like PS2 and Xbox are pushing the videogames industry ever closer to broadcast, with standards rising very quickly.'

'More and more, we're striving for a higher level of in-game artwork,' says Paul Marsden, Human Resources Director at Electronic Arts. 'We've had a number of successful hires bringing people in from film, but really it comes down to a need for good CG and art skills. A good lighting person is a good lighting person, even if real-time 3D does require slightly different thought processes to that for rendered 3D.'

And the games industry is no niche market. Now as lucrative as the movie industry (and growing faster), it sustains dozens of publishers, hundreds of development studios, and thousands of artists. Electronic Arts alone is a $2 billion company, employing 3,800 people worldwide, and currently on a recruitment drive (with many art-based positions available). This continued industry expansion is good news for graduates. Furthermore, the industry offers more low-end positions than film or TV, particularly at larger studios where on-site training is given: 'In those industries, even menial tasks like tracking are quite complex, so there are more opportunities for newcomers,' points out Davenport.

'YOU DON'T EARN AS MUCH IN VIDEOGAMES AS IN FILM OR BROADCAST 3D, BUT THERE ARE CERTAINLY MORE LONG-TERM JOB PROSPECTS.'
Dominic Davenport, ESCAPE STUDIOS

Salaries aren't always very enticing, though. Monica Crisp at agency Change Limited reckons graduates can expect just £12,000–£20,000 at many studios. 'There are a lot of people in the market right now, so employers are more picky, and they want people at knock-down rates. There's a bit of variation, around a couple of thousand pounds between different roles, with modelling probably paying the most.'

That said, Electronic Arts typically offers starting salaries of £20,000–£30,000 plus benefits. 'Last year there was a big demand for animators,' says Marsden. 'This year it's for modellers, lighters, and technical special effects artists. If people can multitask, that's great, but we do tend to recruit people with very strong capabilities in one particular area.'

As vibrant as the games industry is, getting a foot in the door can be incredibly difficult, with up to 50 people chasing every position. And although there's less disparity than ever between rendered 3D and real-time 3D, the gap is still enough to frustrate some artists. 'It's about creating the same sort of effects but within constraints,' says Marsden. 'That requires thinking creatively about how to use their "budget".'

'The creation process requires a better-than-average knowledge of bitmap creation, colour, bits and bytes, and polygon counts,' says Rod Cleasby, a trainer at Metro New Media. 'Animators, in particular, might be sorely disappointed, because so much is put together by the programmers and motion capture guys. Lighting is also a skill you may not practise. And, of course, working on the same project for a year or more isn''t to everyone's taste.'

Surprisingly, an encyclopedic knowledge of games isn't mandatory. 'It is a plus point, but it won't sway a decision if the art skills aren't up to the desired level,' says Marsden. 'What matters more is personality. Teamwork is essential.'

Writing to advise: Activities

Before reading – oral activities

1 **Oral activity for access:**

   a In a pair or in a small group, pick out examples of some of the kinds of advice you have received in your life – for instance, from family members, teachers, friends.

   b Discuss together the kinds of advice which you found helpful, and why.

2 **Oral activity for assessment (individual extended contribution – explain, describe, narrate):**

   a On your own, select an example from the different kinds of advice open to students choosing their sixth-form options – from school, home, libraries, the Internet, etc.

   b Make notes on your chosen advice, how accessible it is, how it is presented and how useful you feel it to be.

   c Give a presentation on your findings, discussing the advice given and how useful it is for a young adult when making these choices.

During reading

When you are advising somebody, you are acting as a friendly expert, giving them the benefit of your knowledge and making suggestions as to what they should do or how they should behave because you think that would be best for them.

1   As you read the extracts in this section, look at:

    - who is being advised (the readership)
    - what is being advised (the topic)
    - how the advice is expressed (the writer's technique).

2   Make brief notes on these three areas, using references
    to and short quotations from the text where appropriate.

3   With a partner or in a small group, pool your findings
    and discuss how appropriate and effective you feel the
    advice to be.

After reading

Select a question from *either* the linked writing *or* the
coursework questions at the end of this book and follow the
instructions to help you prepare and answer the question.

Section 4

Linked writing and coursework activities

The questions which follow are suitable for classwork, homework or timed responses. They are divided into six sections, writing to inform, writing to explain, writing to describe, writing to argue, writing to persuade and writing to advise. Each takes exemplar material from the appropriate section of this book, and then sets out a question based on one of the thematic links running through the book, as set out on page 217.

Writing to inform

Select one or more of the texts you have studied in **Section 1: Writing to inform (page 3)**. Look back at any notes you have made while studying the texts in this section, and spend a few moments reminding yourself of the nature and purpose of information writing. The main aim of information writing is to tell the reader something, giving them the facts about a chosen topic – so it is giving the information clearly which matters here, not the writer's attitudes or feelings. Now choose a question from those listed below.

Remember:
- Always spend time planning your answer before you begin to write.
- Make sure your choice of language is appropriate to the task you have been given.
- Spend some time at the end checking for accuracy of spelling and punctuation.

---

1   **Travel** Study one or more of the texts on the theme of travel listed on page 217 and then complete the following task:

Imagine that you have gone to stay with a family on a school exchange in a different area of the country (choose an area which you know well). It is the evening of your first full day away. Write a letter home to your family informing them about what the town, the house and the people are like.

Remember to:
- put your information in a clear order
- give details
- use the right language for a letter to your family.

2   **Science and technology** Study one or more of the texts on the theme of science and technology listed on page 217 and then complete the following task:

Your local council is very keen that, for security reasons, every elderly person in your local old people's home should have a mobile phone. You have been asked to write an information leaflet for senior citizens on what a mobile phone is, what it can do and how you can use it.

Remember to:
- give your information clearly
- provide facts
- use language appropriate to a mature readership.

3   **Romance** Study one or more of the texts on the theme of romance listed on page 217 and then complete the following task:

Write an article for a teenage magazine informing your readers of the appropriate way to behave when meeting a new friend in a social situation such as a party or disco.

Remember to:
- organise your information clearly
- provide facts
- write in the right language for a teenage magazine.

4   **Growing up**   Study one or more of the texts on the theme of growing up listed on page 217 and then complete the following task:

Write an article for the school newspaper of your local primary school, informing their students about life at secondary school.

Remember to:
- set out your information clearly
- provide details
- use the appropriate language for a primary school newspaper.

5   **Choices**   Study one or more of the texts on the theme of choices listed on page 217 and then complete the following task:

Write an article for the local newspaper, informing their readers about career choices for school leavers in your neighbourhood.

Remember to:
- set out your information clearly
- go into detail
- use the appropriate language for a newspaper article.

Writing to explain

Select one or more of the texts you have studied in **Section 1: Writing to explain (page 31)**. Look back at any notes you have made while studying the texts in this section, and spend a few moments reminding yourself of the nature and purpose of explanation writing. The main aim of an explanation is for the writer to pass their understanding of a topic – an activity, a feeling, a way of behaving – to someone who knows less about it. The writer is the authority, and needs to make their explanation clear, both in the language they use and in the way they organise their material, so that the reader can understand what they are explaining. Now choose a question from those listed below.

> **Remember:**
>
> - Always spend time planning your answer before you begin to write.
>
> - Make sure your choice of language is appropriate to the task you have been given.
>
> - Spend some time at the end checking for accuracy of spelling and punctuation.

1 **Travel** Study one or more of the texts on the theme of travel listed on page 217 and then complete the following task:

Write a leaflet on how to reach your school from the town centre for inclusion in the school prospectus.

Remember to:
- set out your explanation clearly
- give details
- use the appropriate language for a school prospectus.

2 **Occupations** Study one or more of the texts on the theme of occupations listed on page 217 and then complete the following task:

You have been asked by your careers teacher to write an article for the school careers booklet explaining a particular occupation, what the job requires and the qualifications you need.

Remember to:
- explain the different aspects of the job clearly
- provide your reader with details
- write in the right language for a school careers booklet.

3 **Science and technology** Study one or more of the texts on the theme of science and technology listed on page 217 and then complete the following task:

You have a pen pal in a foreign country who is interested in how science education in your country works. Write them a letter, explaining to them how science is studied at your school.

Remember to:
- set out your explanation clearly
- go into detail
- use the appropriate language and layout for a letter to a friend.

4   **War** Study one or more of the texts on the theme of war listed on page 217 and then complete the following task:

A friend of your parents would like you to join the local army cadet group which he runs. Write a letter to him, explaining your views on the army and warfare, and saying why you would or would not like to join.

Remember to:
- organise your explanation clearly
- give details
- use formal language.

5   **Choices** Study one or more of the texts on the theme of choices listed on page 217 and then complete the following task:

Write a letter to your cousin, a Year 9 student, who is going abroad for the first time, explaining to them how to behave in a foreign country.

Remember to:
- set out your explanation clearly
- give details
- use the right language and layout for a letter to a Year 9 student.

Writing to describe

Select one or more of the texts you have studied in **Section 1: Writing to describe (page 46)**. Look back at any notes you have made while studying the texts in this section, and spend a few moments reminding yourself of the nature and purpose of descriptive writing. When writing a description, the writer is trying to paint a picture in the reader's mind, or to conjure up an emotion for them, so that the reader can share in what the writer felt. Now choose a question from those listed below.

Remember:

- Always spend time planning your answer before you begin to write.
- Make sure your choice of language is appropriate to the task you have been given.
- Spend some time at the end checking for accuracy of spelling and punctuation.

---

1   **Occupations**   Study one or more of the texts on the theme of occupations listed on page 217 and then complete the following task:

Describe a day in your life as the school caretaker for the school magazine.

Remember to:
- make your description vivid and lively
- give details of places, people and feelings
- use the appropriate language for a school magazine.

2   **Science and technology**   Study one or more of the texts on the theme of science and technology listed on page 217 and then complete the following task:

Think of a piece of technology which you have enjoyed using – for example, a bicycle, a calculator, a mobile phone. Write a letter to a close friend describing your chosen object and why you like it so much.

Remember to:
- make your description come alive
- include details of the object and of the way you feel about it

- use the right language and layout for a letter to a friend.

3 **Growing up** Study one or more of the texts of the theme of growing up listed on page 217 and then complete the following task:

You have been invited to write a chapter for a new *Handbook for Parents* describing a teenage party. Your chapter is entitled 'The Pleasures and Pitfalls of a Teenage Party'.

Remember to:
- make your description come alive for your readers
- use details of particular events and feelings
- use the right language for an adult audience.

4 **War** Study one or more of the texts of the theme of war listed on page 217 and then complete the following task:

You have recently joined the army, and your regiment has just been posted overseas on a peacekeeping mission. This is the first time you have travelled with your regiment and you are not quite sure what it is going to be like. Write your diary entry for the night before you leave.

Remember to:
- describe events, people and feelings
- give details
- use the appropriate language and layout for a diary entry.

5 **Social issues** Study one or more of the texts of the theme of social issues listed on page 217 and then complete the following task:

The local council has decided to issue a booklet on how to tackle bullying to all schools in the area. You have been asked to contribute an article on 'What it is like to be bullied'.

Remember to:
- make your description come alive for your readers
- give details of events and feelings
- use formal language.

Writing to argue

Select one or more of the texts you have studied in **Section 3: Writing to argue (page 140)**. Look back at any notes you have made while studying the texts in this section, and spend a few moments reminding yourself of the nature and purpose of argumentative writing. When you are writing an argument, you want your reader to end up agreeing with you. You will need to include other, opposing views, but you want to do so in such a way as to make them less convincing than your own view – remember, in the end, that is the view you want to convince your reader is the only right and reasonable view to hold. Now choose a question from those listed below.

> **Remember:**
> - Always spend time planning your answer before you begin to write.
> - Make sure your choice of language is appropriate to the task you have been given.
> - Spend some time at the end checking for accuracy of spelling and punctuation.

1 **Childhood** Study one or more of the texts on the theme of childhood listed on page 217 and then complete the following task:

You have just read a letter to your local newspaper, saying that *'Children today have it too easy!'*. Write a letter to the newspaper in reply, arguing against that point of view.

Remember to:
- give clear reasons for your views

- back up your argument with evidence
- choose the right language and layout for a letter to a newspaper.

2   **Nature** Study one or more of the texts of the theme of nature listed on page 217 and then complete the following task:

Write an article for a popular science magazine arguing that *'human needs are more important than animals'*.

Remember to:
- give clear reasons for your views
- back up your argument with evidence
- write in the appropriate language for a popular magazine.

3   **Travel** Study one or more of the texts on the theme of travel listed on page 217 and then complete the following task:

You work for a travel agent aiming at the student and young adult market. Write an article for their brochure arguing that *'Tourism is a force for good'*.

Remember to:
- give clear reasons for your views
- back up your argument with evidence
- write in the appropriate language for young adults.

4   **Occupations** Study one or more of the texts on the theme of occupations listed on page 217 and then complete the following task:

As an old pupil, you have been invited by your headteacher to put some realism into his pupils' thinking by writing an article for the school newspaper under the title *'There is no such thing as a dream job!'*.

Remember to:
- give clear reasons for your views
- back up your argument with evidence
- select language appropriate to a school newspaper.

5   Science and technology Study one or more of the texts
on the theme of science and technology listed on page
217 and then complete the following task:

You are an ardent campaigner for an ecology group.
Write a leaflet for your group arguing that science and
technology have done more harm than good.

Remember to:
- give clear reasons for your views
- back up your argument with evidence
- choose the right language and layout for a leaflet.

Writing to persuade

Select one or more of the texts you have studied in **Section 3:
Writing to persuade (page 161)**. Look back at any notes you
have made while studying the texts in this section, and spend
a few moments reminding yourself of the nature and
purpose of persuasive writing. When you are writing to
persuade, you want to make your reader behave in a
particular way, even if they had never thought of doing so
before they started to read. Now choose a question from
those listed below.

> **Remember:**
> - Always spend time planning your answer before you
>   begin to write.
> - Make sure your choice of language is appropriate to
>   the task you have been given.
> - Spend some time at the end checking for accuracy of
>   spelling and punctuation.

1   Childhood Study one or more of the texts on the theme
of childhood listed on page 217 and then complete the
following task:

Write an article for a popular magazine, persuading your
readers to visit an area of Britain that you particularly
love.

Remember to:
- make your views clear
- use details to bring your writing alive
- choose the right language for a popular magazine.

2 **Nature** Study one or more of the texts on the theme of nature listed on page 217 and then complete the following task:

You are a campaigner for Greenpeace. Write an article for your local newspaper persuading the local community to pay greater attention to the environment.

Remember to:
- make your views clear
- use details to persuade people you are right
- write in the appropriate language for a local newspaper.

3 **Romance** Study one or more of the texts on the theme of romance listed on page 217 and then complete the following task:

You have been invited by the Minister of Education to submit ideas for a new school curriculum. Write a letter to the Minister persuading them that the discussion of relationships should be a central part of the curriculum. Start your letter '*Dear Minister*'.

Remember to:
- make your views clear
- use details to persuade the Minister that you are right
- use the language and layout appropriate to a formal letter.

4 **Growing up** Study one or more of the texts on the theme of growing up listed on page 217 and then complete the following task:

Write an article for a teenage magazine, persuading readers to support a charity to help young people deal with crisis situations.

Remember to:
- make your views clear
- use details to persuade your readers
- choose the right language for a teenage magazine.

5 **Social issues** Study one or more of the texts on the theme of social issues listed on page 217 and then complete the following task:

There is a gang terrorising the younger children in your school. Write an eye-catching article for your school newspaper persuading them to find a more constructive way of behaving.

Remember to:
- make your views clear
- use details to catch their attention and persuade them you are right
- choose the right language and layout for an article in a school newspaper.

Writing to advise

Select one or more of the texts you have studied in **Section 3: Writing to advise (page 140)**. Look back at any notes you have made while studying the texts in this section, and spend a few moments reminding yourself of the nature and purpose of advice writing. When you are writing to advise, you want to help your reader to make a decision or to act in a way that you think would be helpful for them. Your aim in giving advice is to be clear, authoritative and helpful. Now choose a question from those listed below.

> **Remember:**
> - Always spend time planning your answer before you begin to write.
> - Make sure your choice of language is appropriate to the task you have been given.
> - Spend some time at the end checking for accuracy of spelling and punctuation.

1 **Childhood** Study one or more of the texts on the theme of childhood listed on page 217 and then complete the following task:

You have a friend who has just got a job looking after a toddler at weekends. Write a letter to your friend advising them on ways of looking after the child.

Remember to:
- put your ideas clearly
- be specific – give details
- choose the right language and layout for a letter to a friend.

2 **Nature** Study one or more of the texts on the theme of nature listed on page 217 and then complete the following task:

Write an article for your local newspaper, advising your readers on how to enjoy the natural world in your local area.

Remember to:
- set out your ideas clearly
- give details to back up your recommendations
- write in the appropriate language for a newspaper article.

3 **Travel** Study one or more of the texts on the theme of travel listed on page 217 and then complete the following task:

Write an article for the school magazine, advising younger students on the benefits of foreign travel.

Remember to:
- set out your ideas clearly
- be specific – use details
- use the language appropriate to a school magazine.

4 **Romance** Study one or more of the texts on the theme of romance listed on page 217 and then complete the following task:

A friend is having difficulty forming relationships. Write them a letter of advice so that they will have more success in the future.

Remember to:
- be clear
- give details to back up your recommendations
- use the language and layout appropriate to a letter to a friend.

5 **Choices** Study one or more of the texts on the theme of choices listed on page 217 and then complete the following task:

Write a leaflet for distribution to Year 9 students at your school, advising them on how to make option choices for the years ahead.

Remember to:
- set out your ideas clearly
- give details to back up your recommendations
- use the language and layout appropriate to a leaflet for young adults.

Thematic Links

Childhood:
1.6 'UK Tops Europe for Child Poverty' (p.19)
1.12 'Mummy's Having a Baby' (p.40)
1.14 'The Matron' (p.47)
2.5 'Why TV for Toddlers is Good in Moderation' (p.88)
2.7 *Pants*: My New Book' (p.102)
2.15 'Victoria Climbié' (p.128)
3.3 'Mother's Little Helpers' (p.146)
3.6 'Why Cry?' (p.162)

Nature:
1.9 'Look – A Dinosaur!' (p.32)
1.15 'Far from Shore' (p.49)
2.4 'Going with the Floe' (p.85)
3.9 'Animal Circuses – Animal Suffering' (p.167)
3.15 'Beware of the Geese!' (p.188)

Travel:
1.5 'Mongols and Mare's Milk' (p.143)
1.19 'Jade Eyes' (p.61)
2.9 'New Theroux' (p.106)
3.11 'Myanmar Today' (p.174)
3.14 *Mongolia: A Travel Survival Kit* (p.184)

Occupations:
1.3 'She's Real' (p.9)
1.16 'The Witch' (p.51)
2.10 'Inside Advertising' (p.107)
2.16 *The Political Animal* (p.133)
3.17 'Land Your Dream Job' (p.195)

Science and technology:
1.4 'Patently Good' (p.11)
2.2 'Et in Arcadia Video' (p.77)
2.8 'Science Books for Children' (p.103)
2.13 'Grey Goo' (p.119)
3.13 'Plastic Pollution: It's Everywhere!' (p.181)

Romance:
1.1 'Brand-New Bodies' (p.4)
1.20 'A Chronicle of Love' (p.64)
2.1 'Being 100 per cent sure' (p.73)
3.4 'In Defence of Romance' (p.152)
3.7 'Loving Yourself' (p.163)
3.16 'Give the GIFTS, Avoid the Gaffs' (p.191)

Growing up:
1.11 'Growing Up and Your Feelings' (p.38)
2.6 'The Challenge to Family Life' (p.93)
3.5 'From Crisis to Coping' (p.156)

War:
1.8 Holocaust Resources (p.25)
1.18 'The Girl in the Red Dress' (p.57)
2.3 'Making *Welcome to Sarajevo*' (p.80)
2.11 'Romancing the Holocaust' (p.109)
3.1 'Oxford for Peace' (p.141)
3.10 'Jobs in the Army' (p.172)

Choices:
1.7 'Student Legal Rights' (p.21)
1.13 'Making Choices' (p.41)
2.12 *Sixth Form Choices* (p.115)

Social issues:
1.2 'Policy Statement Against Bullying' (p.6)
1.10 'It's Not Always the Greatest' (p.34)
1.17 'Into the Lion's Den' (p.53)
2.14 *Losing It* (p.122)
3.2 'Supermarkets are bad for your health' (p.143)
3.7 'Work This Out' (p.165)
3.12 'Are You Being Bullied?' (p.179)

Coursework activities

These questions are intended for an extended written response, using texts linked thematically and by genre to enable students to **analyse**, **review** or **comment** on a range of media texts. Remember, this is an opportunity to write clearly, concisely and appropriately on the chosen topic. Two or three sides is enough, as long as every word counts.

1   Study the texts listed below and then complete the task which follows:

   a 'Jade Eyes' (p.61)
   b 'Myanmar Today' (p.174)

   Task: Comment on the views of Myanmar (Burma) put forward in the extracts above. *You can, if you wish, do further research on the country to add substance to your views.*

2   Study the texts listed below and then complete the task which follows:

   a 'Mongols and Mare's Milk' (p.16)
   b *Mongolia: A Travel Survival Kit* (p.184)
   c 'New Theroux' (p.106)

   Task: Using these texts and other examples of travel writing, analyse what it is that, in your view, makes a good piece of travel writing.

3   Study the texts listed below and then complete the task which follows:

   a 'Inside Advertising' (p.107)
   b 'Why Cry?'(p.162)
   c 'Jobs in the Army' (p.172)
   d 'Work This Out' (p.165)

   Task: Comment on at least two advertisements in detail, giving your views on their language and layout, what you feel their aim is and whether you think they achieve it.

4   Study the texts listed below and then complete the task which follows:

    a Holocaust Resources (p.25)
    b 'The Girl in the Red Dress' (p.57)
    c 'Romancing the Holocaust' (p.109)

Task: Comment on the way in which the Holocaust is presented in these texts, and any others you may wish to refer to.

5   Study the texts listed below and then complete the task which follows:

    a 'Policy Statement Against Bullying' (p.6)
    b 'Are You Being Bullied?' (p.179)
    c 'It's Not Always the Greatest' (p.34)

Task: Review these texts, and any others you may wish to refer to, on the way of dealing with bullying, saying what you feel is good or not so good about them, both in terms of content and presentation.

6   Study the texts listed below and then answer the question which follows:

    a 'Myanmar Today' (p.174)
    b 'Oxford for Peace' (p.141)
    c 'Romancing the Holocaust' (p.109)
    d *Losing It* (p.122)

Task: All of the above texts came from websites. Using these and any other websites you may wish to refer to, comment on **at least two** different ways of presenting information on a website, looking at language, layout and any other elements you feel appropriate.

7   Study the texts listed below and then complete the task which follows:

    a 'The Girl in the Red Dress' (p.57)
    b 'Romancing the Holocaust' (p.109)
    c *Schindler's List* (video)

Task: Referring to these three texts in detail, and any others you feel relevant, review Steven Spielberg's treatment of the Holocaust in *Schindler's List*.

8 Study the texts listed below and then complete the task which follows:

  a *Losing It* (p.122)
  b 'Making *Welcome to Sarajevo*' (p.80)
  c *Welcome to Sarajevo* (video)

Task: Referring to these texts and any other films and writings about films you feel relevant, comment on the ways in which ideas are translated into action in film.

Acknowledgements

Every effort has been made to contact copyright holders of material reproduced in this book. Any omissions will be rectified in subsequent printings if notice is given to the publishers.

Scholastic Ltd for an extract from *Horrible Science: The Body Owner's Handbook* by Nick Arnold, published by Scholastic. Text copyright © Nick Arnold, 2002. All rights reserved; Gosford Hill School for School statement against bullying; EMAP for an extract from 'She's Real' by Sylvia Patterson, from *Face* No 69, October 2002; Origin Publishing for '150 years of the Patent Office' by Sally MacArthur, from *Focus* 119, October 2002; The Random House Group Ltd for an extract from *In Search of Genghis Khan* by Tim Severin, published by Hutchinson; News International for 'UK tops Europe for children in poverty' by Simon Vevers, *Nursery World*, 26th September 2002. © Nursery World/TSL Education Ltd, London, 26th September 2002; Guardian Newspapers Ltd for 'Student legal rights: A rough guide' from EducationGuardian.co.uk © Guardian Newspapers Ltd 2003; The Holocaust Memorial Resource and Education Centre of Central Florida for an extract from www.holocaustedu.org/education/index.htm. Text © The Holocaust Memorial Resource and Education Centre of Central Florida, 2001-2002; Michelin Travel Publications for an extract from *I-Spy Dinosaurs and Prehistoric Animals*. Copyright © Michelin 2003. Authorisation No. 0307321; David Higham Associates for an extract from *Letters to Judy: What Kids Wish They Could Tell You* by Judy Blume, published by Heinemann; Usborne Publishing Ltd for an extract from *Understanding the Facts of Life: Part 1 – Growing Up* by Susan Meredith, published by Usborne in 1985. Copyright © 1985 Usborne Publishing Ltd, 83-85 Saffron Hill, London EC1N 8RT; Hamlyn Publishers for an extract from *Siblings* by Dr Richard Woolfson, published by Hamlyn; Terri Apter and W. W. Norton & Company Inc. for an extract from *The Myth of Maturity: What teenagers need from parents to become adults* by Terri Apter, published by W. W. Norton USA in 2001. Copyright © 2001 Terri Apter; David Higham Associates for an extract from *Boy* by Roald Dahl, published by Jonathan Cape Ltd and Penguin Books Ltd; Sort of Books for an extract from *Mapping the Deep: The extraordinary story of Ocean Science* by Robert Kunzig, published by Sort of Books; Amanda Vlietstra and H. Bauer Publishing for 'The Witch' by Amanda Vlietstra, from *Spirit and Destiny*, October 2002; Matthew Weiner for 'Into the Lion's Den' by Matthew Weiner, from *The Big Issue* 7-13 October 2002; Thomas Keneally and The Sayle Literary Agency for an extract from *Schindler's Ark* by Thomas Keneally, published by Serpentine Publishing in 1982. Copyright © Thomas Keneally; The Orion Publishing Group Ltd for an extract from *Stone of Heaven* by Adrian Levy and Cathy Scott-Clark, published by Weidenfeld and Nicholson; Vera Brittain's literary executors, Mark Bostridge and Rebecca Williams, and The Orion Publishing Group Ltd for an extract from *A Chronicle of Youth: Great War Diary 1914-1917* by Vera Brittain; HarperCollins Publishers for an extract from *The 100 Most Asked Questions About Sex, Love and Relationships* by Barbara de Angelis, published by Thorsons. Copyright © Barbara de Angelis, 1997; *The Wire* for 'Et in Arcadia Video' from *The Wire* Issue 224, October 2002; Faber and Faber Ltd for an extract from *Welcome to*

(continued)